LEADERSHIP

SIMON McDONALD was the British ambassador to Germany before becoming permanent under-secretary at the Foreign and Commonwealth Office and Head of HM Diplomatic Service. He sits in the House of Lords as a crossbencher and is master of Christ's College, Cambridge. He is the author of *Beyond Britannia: Reshaping UK Foreign Policy* (2023).

SIMON McDONALD

Leadership

Lessons from a Life in Diplomacy

First published in 2022 by
Haus Publishing Ltd
4 Cinnamon Row
London SW11 3TW

Copyright © Simon McDonald, 2022, 2023

This paperback edition published in 2023

A CIP catalogue for this book is available from the British Library

Cartography produced by Joachim McDonald

Cover shows a detail from 'Foreign Policy', 2016, by Tacita Dean.
Photo: Fredrik Nielsen Studio. Reproduced courtesy the artist and
Frith Street Gallery, London.

The moral right of the author has been asserted

ISBN 978-1-913368-87-6
eISBN 978-1-913368-69-2

Typeset in Sabon by MacGuru Ltd

Printed in the UK by Clays Ltd, Elcograf S.p.A.

www.hauspublishing.com

Contents

Acknowledgements

Early in 2021, after I had left the Foreign Office, a friend asked me what I would do next. I shrugged my shoulders and replied: 'When diplomats retire, they write about their part in historical events. The problem is that, when diplomats describe historical events, they always exaggerate the importance of diplomats, starting with themselves.'

James pondered this for a moment before agreeing that straight autobiography was best avoided. One day my grandchildren might be interested in my version of the events I witnessed, but more people would be interested in an account of how the leaders I saw at close quarters had worked. Could I write about the qualities and behaviours that constituted effective leadership?

Not long afterwards, while scrolling through Twitter, I came across advice from Hemingway's *Death in the Afternoon*: 'The great thing is to last and get your work done, and see and hear and learn and understand; and write when there is something that you know; and not before; and not too damned much after.'

His advice was the final spur. I was a permanent secretary for five years. Permanent secretaries are near the top of the British system, but not quite the peak. If the British system were Everest, I reckon they would be as high as Camp IX, the last overnight staging post before climbers make their final assault on the summit. I enjoyed a good view. So I have written about what I saw on my way to that vantage point.

With thanks to James Bevan for getting me thinking, Ernest Hemingway for getting me writing, and to Olivia for everything else, here's my first book.

Preface

Some days linger a long time in your memory. My first day in the Foreign Office is up there with my first day at school and the birth of each of my children as a moment never to be forgotten. I started work on 6 September 1982. It was a Monday. Although I met life-long friends that day, I find that most details of the day are lost. I remember that I sat between Matthew Kirk and Anna Macey (they married seven years later). I remember asking someone I later discovered was one of the Office's finest negotiators what we did when we realised in a negotiation that the other side's arguments were better than ours. But I do not remember his answer nor most facts about the day.

What lingers longest are my feelings about it. I remember the excitement, the newness, and the effort to remember. I remember liking the people and the surroundings and wanting to make a good impression. I remember one of the two women fast-streamers who joined the year before us bursting with excitement when she told another of her cohort at our welcome reception that the head of the Diplomatic Service knew who she was.

Many years later, I took part in a briefing of permanent secretaries about dementia. The briefer asked us to imagine our memories divided between two bookcases: one was full of events, the other full of feelings; newer memories were stored in the upper shelves. Dementia was like an earthquake rocking the bookcase of events, displacing recent memories rapidly and alarmingly. But the earthquake left the bookcase of feelings unmoved. Memories of recent feelings remained in place (which was why the handling of dementia patients was so important: they might not remember being shouted at, but the reappearance of the person who shouted would trigger alarm).

I hope this doesn't prove to be evidence of early onset dementia but, looking back at my career, how I felt about bosses and colleagues is much clearer in my mind than the details of what they did. So, this book is shaped by those feelings. What worked for me and what did not. What I learnt and how I tried to apply that learning. I have not written a diary since I was a teenager, so I am drawing on partial and possibly wildly inaccurate memories. But I have checked the facts, as far as I can.

Lots of people write about leadership, with academics, businesspeople, football managers, and military officers often at the fore. Why would anyone want to read the thoughts of a retired diplomat? It's a fair question. My immediate answer is that I ran a global organisation, with over 280 outposts in over 170 countries and territories. I worked with six British prime ministers, two of them closely. I observed them do a job that was impossible to do as well as they imagined they would as they climbed Disraeli's 'greasy pole'; they all left office having failed to fulfil their expectations of themselves (the incumbent will join that club in due course). As they clambered to the top, they all developed a rhinoceros hide but were all more wounded by their critics than they cared to admit. I want to write something sympathetic about people doing impossibly difficult but important work. I hope that leaders, aspiring leaders, and those who want to understand how leaders tick might learn something from these personal observations.

Some people might be tempted to pick up this book because of my walk-on part in the fall of Boris Johnson. But, apart from the next three paragraphs and essential changes after the death of Elizabeth II, I wrote the whole of this book before 5 July 2022. In copy-editing, it is true that I had to change one 'Boris Johnson is…' to 'Boris Johnson was…' The book is a long explanation for why I wrote to the Parliamentary Commissioner for Standards on 5 July. Institutions need to defend themselves; if they continue to play by old rules and conventions when a government has ripped up the rule book, they make themselves vulnerable to government caprice.

Everyone I know who worked for Boris Johnson enjoyed the rollercoaster ride for a time, but working for him damaged most of their reputations in the end. Whatever his strengths, Mr Johnson as prime minister was undermining the institutions that define the United Kingdom: Parliament, the Civil Service, the judiciary, the Union itself, and the UK's unwavering respect for international law. In 2022, unease grew as more and more people contemplated the consequences of Mr Johnson's approach to government. My history teacher, K. C. Conroy, taught me the difference between 'cause of' and 'occasion of'. I did not cause Mr

Johnson's downfall. As an anonymous official told *The Sunday Times* on 10 July, 'Boris Johnson is the third prime minister to be brought down by Boris Johnson.' But my tweeted letter and the accompanying interview on Radio 4's *Today* programme were the occasion of his downfall.

My intervention ended with that interview. But I was one of many people to feel the reverberations. Later that day I was told that special advisers in Number 10 were pulling apart my letter line by line, trying to find a flaw. Finding none did not deter them from providing pro-Johnson newspapers with material for disobliging articles about me the next day. My small act of defiance was to tweet 'It's been a good day' after the PM's resignation statement on 7 July. I hope that civility, honesty, and personal responsibility in public life are restored under the new prime minister. The new PM needs to ask, concerning everything the government does, 'Would I mind the king knowing the full story?'

Like many first books, it starts as an autobiography. It ends with my thoughts about the future of different aspects of leadership in the United Kingdom. In between, its main focus is the people – ministers and diplomats – for whom I worked. All my former Civil Service bosses are acknowledged with a footnote the first time their name appears. Assiduous readers of footnotes will work out that in my entire Civil Service career, amounting to twenty-one line managers, I never once had a female boss. Only two women ever countersigned my annual appraisal and only one of them features in the text.* Looking back, the absence

---

* The other was Dame Barbara Woodward DCMG OBE.

of female bosses shocks me: an unlamented feature of a bygone era. From the moment women were allowed to join the Foreign Office in the 1940s they showed they could be expert diplomats, and yet the Board consistently failed to appoint women to senior jobs. By the time I started chairing the Senior Appointments Board (SAB) in 2015, about half of approximately 170 ambassadorial jobs had still been filled only by men. In my time, the SAB appointed women to over fifty ambassadorial jobs never done before by a woman, including Washington, Berlin, Paris, Tokyo and the United Nations in New York. No one at the Foreign, Commonwealth and Development Office will ever work exclusively for male bosses.

Whenever the word 'leader' appears without further explanation, I mean a head of government, cabinet minister, or permanent secretary. But what applies to them often also applies to leaders of small teams, which is why I hope that the readership will be larger than a few dozen people.

1

Role Models

Although I've worked in five different countries, I've had only one employer: the British government. Barriers have been coming down between different parts of the British Civil Service for more than twenty years, but my employer within the British government was specifically the Foreign Office. As someone told my cohort of new entrants in our first week, 'Whenever you have to fill in a form that asks for your employer, for as long as you work here, no matter what your job, write "HM Diplomatic Service".' Which I did for the next thirty-eight years.

Having arrived, I quickly concluded that I wanted to stay. Working for the Foreign Office had long been a vague ambition, the stock answer I gave any adult asking what I wanted to be when I grew up. Not, of course, my first answer. I was a toddler when first posed the question; my mother tells me that I replied, 'I want to be a man.' Later I would routinely answer, 'I want to be a pilot.' But during my teenage years my eyesight deteriorated enough to need glasses and, assuming (erroneously) that you needed 20:20 vision to fly a plane, I cast around for a new ambition.

Being a pilot had seemed the easiest way to see as much

of the world as possible, and that was really my consistent ambition. Both my grandfathers had worked overseas. My father's father had been an engineer working for the White Star Line out of Liverpool, where he'd been born. When he married, he left the merchant navy to be closer to his wife and son – the fact that my dad was nine months old the first time my grandfather saw him sealed his decision. After the Second World War, when he had designed munitions at Woolwich, he joined the brand-new Atomic Energy Authority and eventually rose to be its chief engineer.

My maternal grandfather was the son of a funeral director in Salford. The business and family were housed opposite St James's Church in Pendleton. Everyone assumed, as people did in those days, that an only son would take over the family business. But my grandfather had broader ideas. Although he ran John McDonald & Son (Salford) Ltd for many years, his father having dropped dead of a heart attack in the street while still in his fifties, he wanted to travel.

Grandie's mother was a devout Roman Catholic. The fact that the family home was opposite the parish church significantly helped her routine. She had a weakness for Mediterranean saints. Gerard Majella had provided her son with both his given names, and, as a young woman, she had been infatuated by the story of Our Lady of Fátima as it unfolded in northern Portugal.

In 1917, three peasant children claimed to have seen a vision of a 'lady more brilliant than the sun'. The children reported a prophesy that prayer would bring an end to the Great War. The neighbourhood, and my great grandmother in Salford, convinced themselves that the Virgin Mary had chosen to visit a field in Fátima. As the visions followed a timetable (generally, the 13th of each month) increasingly large crowds gathered to observe the children as they conversed, apparently with thin air.

The vision announced that her last appearance would take place on 13 October 1917, when she would reveal her identity and perform a miracle 'so that all may believe'. Because the children failed to make their August rendezvous (deliberately detained by the local administrator) the lady told the children when they next met that the final proof would be less spectacular than first planned. Some of those present on 13 October at the Cova da Iria failed to see the Miracle of the Sun.

No matter the subsequent controversy in the Vatican, Lúcia and her cousins left a lasting impression on my family. After the birth of his youngest daughter, my grandfather took himself to the registry office and, without consulting my grandmother, named her Jacinta, after the youngest of the three shepherd children. The three of them also prompted Grandie's first independent business venture.

In order to please his widowed mother, Grandie arranged a pilgrimage to Fátima. And in order to pay for both of their passages, he arranged a tour for a group of Catholics. My great grandmother was not the only Salfordian devotee. At the end of the visit (by flying boat from Blackpool to the Douro), he discovered that not only had he been able to pay for himself and his mother, he had also made a profit. He became a travel agent, specialising in pilgrimage travel.

Two grandfathers with multiple stories of abroad, from

Lourdes and Rome to West Africa and the Caribbean, fired my imagination. Casual reading in the dowdy careers office at my grammar school gave it definite shape.

The eponymous brothers founded De La Salle College in a large Victorian house in Weaste in the 1920s. Brother Columba, its first headmaster, wanted his pupils to stand out from the children of other schools. More muted colours for school blazers had already been taken by older schools: bottle green (Salford Grammar), navy blue (Adelphi House), and black (Pendleton High School for Girls). So, he chose cardinal red. The uniform did the job. Teenage boys wearing a distinctive uniform are easily reported to their school when they misbehave.

Among the school's legends is the story of Tony Wilson, who later co-founded Factory Records. In the 1960s, Tony and a posse of boys living in the Stockport area used to take a train and then a bus to get to school (their parents' willingness to inconvenience their children proof that De La Salle was the best Catholic boys' grammar school in southeast Lancashire). On the train they habitually travelled first class, awaiting the arrival and wrath of the conductor before relocating to second class, which their season tickets permitted. One week the conductor lost patience and, having turfed them out of first class for four days running, threatened to inform their headmaster should he find them there the next day. Which he duly did.

When they arrived at Piccadilly station, the boys were escorted meekly to the stationmaster's office and Brother Columba summoned. The headmaster's face clouded as he listened to the conductor's story. Before pronouncing his sentence, he turned to Wilson, the ringleader, and said, 'Well, do you have anything to say for yourself?'

'Yes, Brother. The conductor never asked to see our tickets.' All boys presented first-class tickets to their headmaster, who gave them a lift the rest of the way to school.

Over the years, the original house was joined by a purpose-built main building, a gym, a science block, and a chapel (all since demolished). The careers office was a single room in the Victorian house, with a hardboard floor and metal cupboards and filing cabinets, stocked principally with brochures about universities. Brother Hilary (my headmaster) was proud of the fact that a school whose pupils were 75% working class sent 85% of its sixth-formers to university.

As well as details of undergraduate courses, the room had booklets about a narrow range of careers. As a sixteen-year-old, I read about the Civil Service, including a couple of examples of Foreign Office careers. One was written by a young diplomat from the North of England, who had studied at Keele University. The only other detail I remember after forty-five years is that his first overseas posting was Kabul. My anonymous role model planted a seed.

Some time later, together with everyone in the Upper Sixth, I completed a job aptitude test. Disappointingly, the Foreign Office came second for me behind merchant banking. I asked the teacher why. He told me that diplomacy would have been the perfect career for me but for the answer to one question: 'To what extent would you mind if your career choice impacted on your private life?' I had ticked 'a lot'.

I knew almost nothing about my chosen career, except that it was difficult to get into. Although my role model had studied at Keele, I assumed that studying at Oxford or Cambridge gave a candidate an edge. Despite his pride at the success of his sixth-formers getting into university, Brother Hilary disapproved of Oxbridge: he thought it elitist. But K. C. Conroy, my history teacher, encouraged me to apply to Cambridge, where a student of his had studied law at Pembroke a decade earlier. Having won a place there, I was dismayed when my economics teacher told the class that none of us stood much chance of entering the Civil Service, because the Civil Service recruited overwhelmingly from Balliol, Oxford.

Undaunted by that lingering factoid, I applied to the Civil Service and in the spring of 1982 found myself in the Corn Exchange at Cambridge, along with what seemed like the entire complement of third-year students, sitting the Civil Service entrance exam. As required to proceed further, I passed both halves: English/General Knowledge and Maths/Science. In the three intervening years, my ambition to join the Foreign Office had solidified. I was a child of Butler and Beveridge. My parents paid their taxes but made no other financial contribution to my education from the age of four to twenty-one. Giving back and public service appealed strongly.

The final encouragement was learning that a historian from Pembroke in the year ahead of me had won a fast-stream place. 'Well, he's not that clever,' I thought, based on almost no evidence. His success led me to apply only for HM Diplomatic Service. I chose not to seek a back-up option in the Home Civil Service, Inland Revenue, or Hong Kong Civil Service (it was fifteen years before the handover).

Instead, my back-up plan was a couple of applications to merchant banks. I had a final interview with the Hongkong and Shanghai Banking Corporation (HSBC). In those days, the chairman saw final-round applicants in his sumptuous office on Poultry in the City of London. After half an hour's general chitchat, he observed from my application that the other area of work that interested me was the Foreign Office. He asked which job I would choose if offered both HSBC and FCO. Unhesitatingly, I replied, 'The FCO.' He looked as if I had slapped him in the face.

My Final Selection Board for the FCO was a happier experience and, on 5 August 1982, I was offered a job as a Grade 8 in the fast stream.

The most alarming thing about my first day was the journey to work. The parents of a university friend had offered me a bed for my first few days in London. They lived in Hillingdon. As I sat on the Metropolitan line tube, I found it difficult to imagine that anyone, still less millions of people, might subject themselves to a twice-daily commute of over sixty minutes.

Arriving at Palace Chambers, I felt expected. And the building reminded me of school: draughty, dark, leaky, and noisy. It shook every time a District or Circle line train passed through Westminster station. Like my school, it has since been demolished, replaced by Portcullis House. The person at reception had my name on a list. Evidence that I am in the right place is always a comfort. (On my first day at university, I was impressed to find my name painted at the bottom of 'X' staircase of Orchard Building: paint meant there could be no mistake.) On our first FCO afternoon, my group of new entrants was assigned our jobs for the next year. Two of us headed to the Western European Department (WED), where I would be Benelux desk officer and the other new entrant, James Bevan, would work on the Council of Europe and Western European Union. We met Rob Young,* the assistant head of department, who introduced us to our section heads, who were also our line managers.

The rest of our four-day induction is hazy. At the time, it seemed more important to get to know the other new entrants than to absorb what the string of senior and junior briefers had to say. We learned about telegrams, distributed three times per day, pink for outgoing (all signed by Francis Pym, the foreign secretary) and white for incoming (all signed by whoever was in charge of the mission) the fiction being that diplomatic communications were conducted between the foreign secretary direct with ambassadors. We also had a scattering of green telegrams, traffic from European Economic Community states shared with other member states. The content of the green telegrams was either technical or inane.

One session of our induction, which eighteen years later I had to be persuaded had happened, concerned pensions. When you join any organisation, you do not know which information your new employer shares early on will matter most later. But, no matter how young you are, pay attention

---

* Sir Rob Young GCMG.

to your pension. In 1982 employees of the FCO were automatically part of the Civil Service's 'classic' scheme; the name was attached years later when it was replaced by the 'alpha' scheme. The energy the Office put into convincing colleagues that they should switch persuaded me to stick with the classic, which turned out to be the better decision for my personal circumstances.

But, as alpha was being rolled out, I worked out that I would never be able to earn a full pension. Classic was calculated on forty years' service. Yet until 2011 it was almost impossible for my cohort to rack up forty years: to be a fast-streamer you needed an Honours degree (and few graduates from British universities were younger than twenty-one) and everyone was turfed out of the Civil Service at sixty. In earlier times, you could earn pension benefits at one-and-a-half times time-served in some hardship posts, but that perk had been scrapped by the time I took an interest. The solution to filling the gap was to buy added years, which you paid for every month until you retired. The longer you delayed the purchase, the more you had to pay each month.

Apparently, this was all explained in my first week. But, as an indebted twenty-one-year-old earning £400 per month, I was more interested in my new colleagues than the details of our pension. There were eighteen of us, fourteen men and four women. Fourteen had studied at Oxbridge, including one who had studied at both Oxford and Cambridge. We were all white. Eventually we all married, apart from the one who resigned, having come out in his late twenties (the FCO dropped the bar on employment of LGBT+ people only in 1992).

Most of us spent the majority of our careers at the FCO. A couple left after their first posting, one transferring to the Home Civil Service, another to the private sector. Eight eventually became ambassadors or high commissioners. Comparing notes years later, one of the strongest markers for how long we stayed and how high we rose was our experience in our first year: colleagues who liked and admired their bosses in their first year did better professionally. The Office had always designated certain jobs as training jobs, real but not consequential enough for the holder accidentally to cause a diplomatic incident. The Office paid more attention to the jobs than who was line-managing those jobs. Certainly, in 1982/3, it did not feel to some of us that our line managers' performance training new entrants weighed heavily in their annual appraisal.

I was fortunate. My first boss was Nicholas Armour,* head of section for France. Nicholas was a nice man who had just married an even nicer wife. I later worked out that he treated me exactly like a head of chancery used to treat a new third secretary: he treated me like a member of his extended family, inviting me to his house and advising on every aspect of life in the Office.

I am a chameleon. Looking back, I recognise a need always to fit in. Looking around the Office in 1982, I saw that was a straightforward task for a white man with a Cambridge degree and a ready-to-read-the-news accent. I spotted the facts that most people's suits had seen better

---

* Nicholas H. S. Armour.

days and nearly everyone wore shiny Oxford shoes. Nicholas later told me that Rob and he had been amused to see James and me wearing only plain white shirts as if they were part of a uniform. I quickly branched out into Bengal stripes and braces.

I never felt that I did not belong or that the Office had made a ghastly error in admitting me. Imposter syndrome was not a thing in the 1980s but, even in retrospect, it does not fit my feelings. The selection process had been protracted enough to make a mistake seem implausible. I wanted to do well, and to do well I reckoned I needed to fit in. Aged twenty-one, my authentic self was not developed. I wanted to do good, help others, and leave things better than I found them. I wanted to do the right thing and make my family and teachers proud. And that was about it. Fitting in did not feel like compromising anything important.

Together with Rob Young, Nicholas drilled me in the basics, taught brevity, clarity, and accuracy, preached the importance of meeting deadlines (despite his evident difficulty in meeting his own standard) and consulting everyone with a legitimate interest, who were to be given a reasonable time to respond but who were also to understand that their silence at that point would not delay the progress of a piece of work up the system. Rob once told me that it had taken him seven years to learn the FCO written style, which puzzled as much as daunted me (we were not learning to write Mandarin). When later I retold the story, I realised that I could not pinpoint when I (nor, indeed, the Office) was satisfied with my style.

Andrew Wood,* the head of WED, floated benignly above us. I noticed that his letters were always short and his eyes always smiling: the former achievement meant everyone knew what he thought about everything he cared about; the latter meant everyone liked him. He once showed me great confidence and kindness. I had got drunk on champagne at a reception at the Victoria and Albert Museum. Asked to carry one of the exhibits by the friend organising the exhibition whose launch we were celebrating, I damaged it. The friend's boss was furious and complained to my boss that a cartoon had been scratched. I paid for its repair. Afterwards, Andrew took me aside for a fatherly discussion, of the sort fathers give when they have instructions to impart, which they are more than usually confident their sons will accept because of the circumstances requiring the discussion. I have never had a two-day hangover since.

One of Nicholas's smaller responsibilities was Monaco. A few weeks after my arrival in WED, Princess Grace died in a car crash. Nicholas had to write a couple of messages of condolence and arrange British attendance at the princess's funeral. No one pretended that the late princess had been a political player or that her funeral would be a chance to conduct diplomatic business. But she was popular, and the world's media were vigilant for slights and official insensitivity. Eventually it was decided that the Princess of Wales should represent the United Kingdom.

The messages were boilerplate: short, warm, uncontroversial. But it struck me that even the simplest and most

---

* Sir Andrew Wood GCMG.

obvious official communication had to start somewhere. The point was to produce something serviceable quickly, make sure that everyone with an interest knew what was going on, and leave room for the person signing the message to personalise it.

I learned quickly that, although outsiders often assume that senior reaches of hierarchy tinker with the work of more junior colleagues, much work passes through the system unchanged. When the prime minister of the Netherlands resigned, I wrote a simple message from Margaret Thatcher wishing him well. The head of chancery (head of political section) in the Hague was shocked that the British prime minister should address her departing Dutch colleague by his nickname ('Dear Dries, indeed'), a personal touch I had included without consulting anyone.

Nicholas schooled me in office gossip. One day, when an imposing and utterly bald man stuck his head around the door asking to know the whereabouts of our head of department, Nicholas told me, 'That's Patrick Wright.* People say he was a brilliant ambassador to Syria, even though not a single one of his political predictions came true. People also say he'll be our next PUS and head of the Diplomatic Service.'

Before joining the Foreign Office, I had never heard of a PUS (P.U.S.). I soon learned that the one thing that distinguishes FCO people is that they can see and say those three letters without thinking of oozing bodily fluids. These days all other departments call their top civil servant the

---

* Lord Wright of Richmond GCMG.

permanent secretary – only the Foreign, Commonwealth, and Development Office sticks to permanent under-secretary. The title is a relic of history and reflects the Office's structure when it was first established.

In March 1782, at the start of an administration that lasted just ninety-seven days, Lord Rockingham reorganised Whitehall departments. Until then, both the old Northern and Southern Departments had dealt with aspects of foreign policy. From then on, all overseas policy was consolidated into the Foreign Office and domestic policy into the Home Office (formally the more senior of the two). Both departments were small, headed by a secretary of state, and these were the only secretaries of state in the cabinet. Charles James Fox began the first of three brief stints at the Foreign Office that year. To commemorate him as the first ever foreign secretary, John Kerr* (PUS, 1997–2002) placed a bust of Fox on a table at the foot of the Grand Staircase in Downing Street West. Fox's deputy was called under-secretary of state (the 'of state' is still part of the full title).

As the world occupied more of the government's time, so an extra under-secretary was introduced. In the early nineteenth century, the men holding these offices changed whenever the government changed. Not until the 1830s did one of the under-secretaries argue that someone (himself) should stay on to ensure continuity between administrations.

When his proposal was accepted, the two office holders became known as the permanent under-secretary and the

---

* Lord Kerr of Kinlochard GCMG.

parliamentary under-secretary, a junior minister to help the secretary of state deal with business in Parliament. Until the Second World War, whenever a new department was created, it was launched with the Home Office/Foreign Office structure.

At some point, other departments rebelled. The PUS title was not particularly clear outside of its nineteenth-century context. Although some other countries had adopted it (mostly Commonwealth but also Bulgaria), for the most part it confused outsiders. The key attribute to convey in a revised title was continuity when ministers changed whole-sale after a general election. Although 'secretary' was also confusing, it was less objectionable than 'under'. Despite occasional interest in adopting the French model (secre-tary-general), 'permanent secretary' has stuck.

Antony Acland* had been PUS for five months when I joined. Patrician, diligent, and foul-tempered, he looked indistinguishable from the portraits of his predecessors, which hung on the wall of his private secretaries' office. My contemporaries claim that he gave us sherry at the reception his office organised on our first day. I do not remember that, but I do remember him surveying us and asking, 'Which one of you is Jock's boy?' Until then, Duncan Taylor had managed to avoid sharing the fact that his father was ambassador to the Federal Republic of Germany.

Apart from a reception of disputed memory, I had no contact with Antony in my first year and little contact after-wards. But without ever considering what a PUS should

---

* Sir Antony Acland KG GCMG GCVO.

look like, I immediately accepted that he looked the part: thin, precise, immaculately tailored. Nicholas said that Julian Bullard* had been Lord Carrington's choice (he had resigned as foreign secretary shortly after the announcement of Antony's appointment) but Mrs Thatcher had preferred Antony, suspicious of someone else's recommendation.

Nicholas encouraged me to get to grips with the structure and history of the Office. I learned about the Plowden and Duncan Reviews: Plowden preceded the merger of the Foreign Office and Commonwealth Relations Office in 1968; Duncan led to an increased emphasis on commercial and trade work for the new Foreign and Commonwealth Office (a hardy perennial of a policy, but beginning with Duncan).

I saw the impact of the merger in the layout of the building. Next to the office I shared with Nicholas was a narrow dog-leg-shaped corridor, known as the Hole in the Wall. The corridor had been carved out of the colonial secretary's ministerial suite. What had been the colonial secretary's office, renamed the Map Room, was dominated by a custom-built, burr walnut display case, which still retained the maps it was designed to store (since transferred to the National Archives).

Our corridor was the second most splendid in Downing Street West, where the deputy secretaries had traditionally been housed to give them easy access to the foreign secretary and ministers in the most splendid corridor. By 1982, most of the huge nineteenth-century offices had been

---

* Sir Julian Bullard GCMG.

sub-divided, but we retained one deputy secretary, whose job title had recently been renamed (to align with his opposite numbers in the EEC). Julian Bullard was the FCO's first 'political director'.

Julian had high cheek bones, sunken eyes, and Bobby Charlton hair. He looked simultaneously forbidding and careless of his appearance. He had the reputation of being the cleverest person working for the Foreign Office. I hadn't a clue how to talk to him. The first-week instruction to call everyone by their first name, apart from the PUS and our own head of mission (recently downgraded from 'Excellency' to 'Ambassador'), did not help at all. I called him nothing; I was gruntled when he called me Simon.

Julian modelled not so much hard work as effective work. Everything in which he took an interest, he shaped. He focussed on where he believed he needed to make a difference. As well as being unfailingly polite when he had reason to be cross, he taught two specific lessons in two short one-to-one meetings. The political director from one of my countries visited him. As desk officer, I provided part of the briefing and attended the meeting to take a note. A couple of hours after I had submitted my draft, Julian called me in (my office was opposite his). He handed back my draft. Large sections had been crossed out; others had been replaced with small but legible handwriting. He said something along the lines of: 'Thank you. I know you haven't taken many records and this was your first for me. It's perfectly accurate. But your job is not to take a verbatim record. Your job is simply to record points of interest or requiring action in unambiguous language.'

A subsequent effort dismayed Julian sufficiently for him to call me in again. He lamented the fact that English grammar was no longer taught in schools and showed me how to write indirect speech: 'The reconciliation of tenses may sometimes seem illogical, but overall its discipline and consistency make any document easier to understand.' (I confess the quotations are invented but I hear them in his voice.)

The second grandest person on our corridor was Alan Goodison,* assistant under-secretary for Europe. He looked happy to be sandwiched between an abler deputy and an even abler boss. He was observant, kindly, and calculatedly indiscreet. One morning Nicholas was shocked to read some policy development in a newspaper and slightly more shocked in the afternoon when Alan told him that he had placed the story. He was the first exponent I knew of Whitehall's favourite irregular verb: I brief, you leak, he or she breaks the Official Secrets Act.

My main dealing with Alan was arranging the visit of Pierre Werner, Luxembourg's prime minister. The programme included a call on Margaret Thatcher. Alan represented the FCO at that meeting. Later he told me that just four people had been present: the two prime ministers, the Luxembourg ambassador, and himself. He felt he had done a reasonable job in covering up the awkwardness of our prime minister sleeping through most of the meeting.

By far the most elaborate visit I was involved in during my first year was the state visit of Queen Beatrix, who had

---

* Sir Alan Goodison KCMG CVO.

recently succeeded her mother as queen of the Netherlands. Preparations were in full swing when I turned up in September, but a couple of outstanding tasks fell to the new desk officer. I had to compile a guest list for the state banquet at Buckingham Palace and contribute to the guest list for the Lord Mayor's Banquet at Guildhall. Nicholas told me that I could put myself on the latter.

My most imaginative recommendation was Ernie Wise for Guildhall. He was invited and his presence was noted in the papers. Apparently, he had been taken aback by the occasion, having expected a show-business vibe; he could not account for his invitation. I had included him because I had read somewhere that he was a well-known clog dancer.

My larger task was writing the first draft of the speech the queen was to deliver at the state banquet. I read a few earlier examples and set to work. My draft passed unscathed out of the department and was cleared without comment by Alan and Julian. The foreign secretary thought it dwelt overly on the historical relationship and so some extra references to business were added, and off it went to the other end of the Mall. When the visit was over, the queen's private secretary phoned Rob to thank whoever had written it, one of the nicer notes on my INDIV (personnel) file.

A few weeks later the Office celebrated the 200th anniversary of the establishment of the office of foreign secretary. The anniversary had fallen in March but preparations for the Falklands War led to a postponement of the queen's visit to unveil a plaque. The monarch's November visit was planned in minute detail. Her Majesty would look into a couple of the offices on the route from the Downing Street

West entrance to the foreign secretary's office. Nicholas and I were on the route.

On the day, the mistress of the robes informed the queen that I was the young man who had produced the first draft of the Netherlands speech. On reflection, I think it was unnecessary to inform Her Majesty that the speech was the first I had ever written.

My first year passed quickly. I paid off my debts, which at one point oppressively hit £650. At that point, I received a statement for my first credit card, informing me that the minimum monthly payment was £10. Because I could not afford £10, I paid nothing. I then received a tart letter explaining what minimum payment meant. In order to reduce living expenses, I moved flat twice. After a week in Hillingdon, I shared a flat with a university friend and one of his friends, who – it turned out – did not much like me. I next took a one-bedroom flat over an antiques shop in Kensington Church Street. It was by far my grandest London address but ruinously expensive and haunted by the landlady through whose maisonette I had to tramp, too noisily, she informed me, giving me notice to quit after only six months.

Sight unseen, I took a flat in a house owned by the father of another university friend. The friend and his girlfriend were in the downstairs flat. No one had seen the inside of the first-floor flat for years when the tenant suddenly upped sticks. My friend's father adjusted the rent downwards when he saw how much work his next tenant was taking on. My brother Dominic moved in to help with the refurbishment and to look for a job in London. He was gay, and London felt more promising than Salford as a place where he would find congenial colleagues. He quickly found a job as a window dresser and almost as quickly displaced the girlfriend downstairs.

The most consequential decision the Personnel Operations Department (POD) took about me in my first year was related to which so-called 'hard language' I should learn. There was a consultation: my whole cohort was asked which half-dozen languages we might consider. At number six I put Arabic. Nicholas had studied Arabic and worked in Beirut; he had enjoyed it and I needed to fill in the sixth box. Later I informed POD that I had changed my mind. They asked why and I replied, 'Because I can't imagine asking a woman who agrees to marry me to move to Saudi Arabia.'

Some time later, I was on a course with most of my cohort. As the week wore on, I became aware that everyone else was hearing about their second-year assignment, and getting a posting or language they wanted, apart from me. On the Friday I phoned POD and was informed airily, 'It's not your first choice. You're going to learn Arabic before being posted to Jeddah.' Even as a respectful twenty-two-year-old, I was stung into replying, 'You're dead right it's not my first choice; it's the only posting I told you I actively did not want.'

I accepted my fate. I was never a good Arabic speaker and needed two attempts to pass the intermediate exam, only the second exam I had ever failed (having written about Louis XI instead of Louis IX in my History Special Level; to this day, I use Roman numerals when writing dates as a small reminder of my mistake).

After spending a couple of days with Nicholas in Athens, where he was head of chancery, I arrived in Jeddah in May 1985. Soberly, I refused offers of alcohol on the Olympic Airways flight, believing I had to get used to a dry life. So I was astonished to discover that the diplomats in Saudi Arabia were even more marinated in alcohol than students. I was also astonished by the heat and humidity, which had a ferocity I had believed could only exist concentrated into a small space, like an oven.

I was serving in Saudi Arabia when the embassy moved from Jeddah. The Al Saud's capital, Riyadh, had traditionally been closed to foreigners. When King Abdul Aziz united the country and established its present borders in the first decades of the twentieth century, it suited him to keep the diplomatic corps in the port city of Jeddah, the traditional gateway to Mecca and Medina, where foreigners were commonplace. The arrangement suited the first three of his sons who followed him as king. But when Fahd became king in 1982, his full brother, Salman, governor of Riyadh, lobbied for the corps to move to the capital. King Fahd decreed that all embassies should relocate to Riyadh from September 1985. Helping to move the embassy was my first big task.

Patrick Wright was my first ambassador. Apart from assuming that my Arabic was better than it was, he was a wonderful boss: generous, energetic, and stretching. I have wanted to please all my bosses, but pleasing Patrick became an obsession. He was so grateful and encouraging, and his contentment with one completed task meant the next would be more demanding. He loved to answer questions and to explain things, about Saudi Arabia and the intricate connections between the men running the place, about the Office, about the Arabic language, and about the history of Britain's involvement in the Middle East for starters. He was basically interested in everything.

And he was determined, without ever saying it out loud, to be the best ambassador to Saudi Arabia – both the best in the corps and the best compared with British predecessors, whose portraits hung in the stairwell of the new embassy building. His toughest competition was his immediate predecessor, James Craig, famously the FCO's best-ever Arabic scholar. James dealt with, and did not enjoy, the fallout from the BBC's broadcast of *Death of a Princess* – he comforted himself with the thought that every British ambassador's mission in Saudi Arabia was defined by a crisis not of their own making.

Patrick refused to be daunted, or even acknowledge, the caprice of senior Saudi princes. He accepted appointments, no matter when or where proposed. During Ramadan, that could be in the middle of the night; during the summer, in Taif; at any time, in Riyadh when we were living in Jeddah, and in Jeddah after we had moved to Riyadh.

Patrick was more fortunate than James: the defining event of his mission to Saudi Arabia was the signing of the Al Yamamah contract, the sale of Tornado fighters to the Royal Saudi Air Force, which at the time was the biggest defence sale ever made by the UK. The Saudis insisted on a government-to-government contract, which meant the ambassador could not be excluded, even if it would have suited British Aerospace (BAe), the main British contractor, to do so. Saudi Arabia and its defence industry are notoriously corrupt (in 2019 Crown Prince Mohammed bin Salman detained some of the wealthiest members of his family until they surrendered a portion of their ill-gotten gains). My hazy assumptions about the prevalence of corruption were confirmed when a potential Saudi customer explained to me exactly what had to happen if the contract we were discussing were to go Britain's way. I saw Patrick. He said it was a straightforward matter: we never did anything corrupt; the standard was absolute and easy to understand. Once we deviated, matters quickly stopped being straightforward and started being illegal.

I used to think that Patrick's integrity was an impediment to corruption on both sides. Now I am not so sure. I suspect corrupt parties sheltered behind his iron-clad integrity. No one would ever accuse him of anything improper, but the deal was simply too big for him to know all its details.

The two counsellors in the embassy were Andrew Green* (Riyadh's first deputy head of mission, a new job in the Diplomatic Service, the duties of which subsumed most of what a head of chancery used to do) and Jeremy Greenstock† (commercial counsellor). They complete my roster of early role models. Flinty, focussed, and ambitious, they had more in common than they cared to admit. I never heard either say a bad word about the other, but neither took trouble to disguise their antipathy. Patrick's solution was to ignore the problem, which was fair enough as Andrew and Jeremy

---

* Lord Green of Deddington KCMG.
† Sir Jeremy Greenstock GCMG.

were scrupulously collegiate in his presence. And it was a successful solution: in the building everyone took their cue from Patrick. The place hummed contentedly.

Patrick's departure from Riyadh in May 1986 to become PUS marked the end of my first phase in the Foreign Office. From then on, I was no longer new. My first phase was fortunate: all my bosses were kind and everyone around me helped me do my job better. I learned by osmosis. Over the years I have found out more about my early bosses. I am struck by how many suffered personal tragedy (details of which are not mine to share); their overcoming of adversity may have been part of what made them good to work for and learn from.

One personal story – more of adversity than tragedy – I can share is Julian's. In Britain you can acquire social status in a single generation. Reader Bullard, Julian's father, was the UK's first ambassador from a working-class background. Julian's grandfather had been a labourer in the East End who left behind just £10 when he died. The grandfather had encouraged his brightest child to study. With determination and scholarships, Reader passed the exams to join the Consular Service in 1908. The possibilities at the end of his career opened up when the Consular Service merged with the Diplomatic Service in 1933. He became minister at Jeddah and then ambassador at Tehran during the Second World War. He organised Winston Churchill's sixty-ninth birthday party in November 1943, when Churchill sat between Marshal Stalin and President Roosevelt (the glittering placement is preserved in silver outside the dining room of the Ambassador's Residence in Tehran).

Julian's mother was the daughter of Arthur Smith, Master of Balliol (six of whose seven daughters married knights), but the East End was the key to understanding him. Good people are found everywhere. We should assume that everyone we meet is good, no matter how humble their background or how different from our own. Talented people are rarer than good people, but they too are found everywhere. A sensible society seeks out and encourages talent wherever it is found.

Management theories were less developed in the 1980s. Without anyone uttering the words 'presumed competence' it was clear that that was how we were all treated. Without anyone talking about, still less offering to be, a mentor, it was clear I benefited from a string of first-class mentors. We never had a structured career conversation, but we had countless interesting conversations about everything under the sun.

I was surprised when Patrick became PUS. Although I was delighted to be surrounded by excellence, it never occurred to me that these colleagues were the best the Office had to offer. I assumed that everyone else, the numberless colleagues I had never met, was just as good or better. I experienced the same surprise seeing actors at university achieve world renown. Emma Thompson, Tilda Swinton, Stephen Fry, Hugh Laurie, and Sandi Toksvig were wonderful undergraduate entertainers; it never occurred to me that they might be the best in their generation. We are blasé about what is familiar.

After Patrick's appointment, I asked a visitor from London why he got the PUS job. He replied: 'Energy! The man never says no. He inspires confidence. He makes you believe that whatever he says he'll do, he'll do, and whatever he says will happen, will happen.'

I believe that setting out on the right path is important, especially when you are young. It is not always easy to see which is the right path. I remember an undergraduate discussion about Moses Finley's contention that Rome imported the seeds of its downfall from Greece. By copying the Greeks' reliance on enslaved people in their economy, the Romans, like the Greeks, failed to develop technologically. Who you choose as your guide has consequences later.

I see now (though I did not at the time) the limitations of my mentors and role models: all men, all white, all working for one hidebound organisation, but mostly, I think, aware of those limitations and keen to challenge them. The FCDO looks different today partly because of their efforts. One reason the mentors and the role models at the beginning of my career were so useful in setting standards and aspirations was because they were the organisation's best.

2

Indifferent Models

Memory unaided by documents loses subtlety. My first bosses and managers were not heroes all the time. But where my memory is incomplete or hazy, I give them the benefit of the doubt. Similarly, the next group were not miserable martinets: they were exceptional diplomats, just less congenial colleagues for me.

Stephen Egerton* boasted that he was the latest in a long line of public servants, stretching back to the eighteenth century. He claimed kinship with the Dukes of Bridgewater. I knew that he could not be descended from the third duke, who built the first canals in Salford, because Francis Egerton had no children and the title died with him. Public service had generally rewarded Stephen's ancestors, but the honours he sought seemed to have been snatched from him when we met in Riyadh in 1986. He was accompanying the foreign secretary, Geoffrey Howe. In the embassy, we were agog to know who would succeed Patrick, whose appointment as PUS had just been announced.

We all knew that Stephen had been posted to and was

_____
* Sir Stephen Egerton KCMG.

much looking forward to Mexico City. Later that summer, Mexico was hosting the FIFA World Cup. Although Stephen was not a football fan, he was looking forward to senior British focus on his posting, one of a large group of countries whose importance is clearer to British diplomats than to British ministers. We wondered whether Stephen might be diverted from Mexico City to Riyadh, because everyone agreed on the key importance of Saudi Arabia to British interests. Stephen's presence in Geoffrey Howe's party was unremarkable: he was assistant under-secretary responsible for the Middle East but, once the party was ensconced in Riyadh's Guest Palace, he made a beeline for the Ambassador's Residence. He made it plain that he wanted to inspect his new home.

Stephen's conversation was reliably divided into three unequal parts: (i) profanities, (ii) inappropriately warm terms of endearment (it was disconcerting to be addressed as 'my dear' until you realised he called everyone 'my dear'), and (iii) shrewd analysis or precise instruction. I do not know if he originated the observation, but everyone who worked for him quotes him telling a minister who thought it time to shift the UK's foreign policy focus that , 'You can ignore the Middle East if you want to, but you mustn't be surprised if the Middle East doesn't ignore you for long.'

Stephen strove to improve relations between the House of Saud and the House of Windsor. The Al Saud had ruled the Nejd (central Arabia) with interruptions for almost 300 years but Abdul Aziz expanded their lands into the Hejaz in 1925, his conquest ending 700 years of Hashemite rule. Now controlling most of the Arabian Peninsula, he accepted the title of 'king' in 1926. His son, Prince Sultan, minister of defence, told me that foreign pilgrims, visiting Mecca for the annual pilgrimage, had forced the hand of local sheikhs, insisting that they offer his father the throne of Hejaz. By the 1980s, four of Abdul Aziz's sons had succeeded him as king. The family appeared secure on its throne but, by taking it in turns, observing strict seniority and remaining king until death, new kings were becoming older and older when they took over. More than thirty years after Abdul Aziz's death, the Al Saud had still not addressed the problem of choosing a king from among his proliferating grandsons. Seeking to consolidate the rule of the new royal house, senior members of the House of Saud were fascinated by the staying power and stability of the House of Windsor.

Stephen called the score of King Abdul Aziz's surviving sons 'valetudinarians', old men whose main ambition was to grow older. In this quest, other people's inconvenience did not signify. Prince Naïf (minister for the interior) offered Stephen a series of nocturnal times in remote destinations for their introductory call – he turned them all down. 'Please explain to His Royal Highness's office that, as a man in his fifties, I need to sleep in the middle of the night and, unlike my predecessor, I am simply not prepared to travel eighteen hours for a twenty-minute appointment, no matter how august my host.' The ministry offered a daytime meeting in the prince's Riyadh office within a week.

In 1987, the Prince and Princess of Wales visited Riyadh and Jeddah and the Saudis went over the top to demonstrate their affection. Stephen took a minute interest in the programme, determined to preserve time for Her Royal Highness to 'prink', 'A much more economical word, Simon, to put in print than "to rest and change clothes".' Because of his closeness to Syria, Crown Prince Abdullah felt the need to react to the recent break in diplomatic relations between London and Damascus; he disappeared from the kingdom shortly before Their Royal Highnesses' arrival. Stepping in to act as host, Prince Sultan, second deputy prime minister and minister of defence, was determined that no slight should be felt. His office's final enquiry, the evening before Their Royal Highnesses' arrival, was to ask what temperature the princess would like her swimming pool. Presents were generous and unmistakably Saudi, including Arabian horses, a canteen of solid silver cutlery stamped with the Saudi crest, and a large gold falcon standing on a malachite base.

Because men and women socialise separately in Saudi, the princess had a separate programme. But King Fahd was determined to meet the most famous young woman in the world. Before the state banquet at his new Al Yamamah Palace (the first function to be held there), he insisted on an audience with both guests. The princess was the only woman in a huge reception room, filled with princes and cabinet ministers. Every man in the kingdom who counted was there. The Princess of Wales wore a long white dress by the Emanuels. For the whole time she was present, she was the only object of attention; the king was clearly reluctant to release her to the parallel banquet given by his favourite wife.

Once we moved to the banqueting hall, I was intrigued

to see that only the British guests had name plates to mark their place. Because there were so few of us, we sat between the most senior Saudis. I asked my neighbour why his name plate said only 'sahib al-samu al-malaki al-amir...'. He explained that seating was strictly in protocol order. Every prince knew his seniority by age in the family. So, at the start of any function a prince would look around to check who else from the family was there. A prince did not need to know all 5,000 princes, just the dozen or so born around the same time as himself. By the time they moved into dinner all princes knew where to sit, so needed to be guided only by 'His Royal Highness Prince...' to get to the right place.

The following year King Fahd paid a state visit to the UK. The Saudis were delighted by his treatment. Their only slight unhappiness was caused by the awards they did and did not receive. The king accepted the Royal Victorian Chain (an honour largely reserved for visiting heads of state and retiring archbishops of Canterbury) despite the fact that its insignia includes a prominent cross, which the religious in Saudi Arabia thought an inappropriate adornment for their monarch. The king's suite included senior ministers (who were made Knights Grand Cross) and his favourite son. Prince Abdul Aziz was tall for his age, but no one pretended he was eighteen years old. Government policy held firm: awards were never conferred on minors and the prince would be no exception.*

---

* The queen changed the rules twenty-one years later when Ellie Simmonds was awarded an MBE aged fourteen for her achievements at the Beijing Paralympic Games.

At the end of 1987, the Personnel Department put me forward for a place on the international course at the École nationale d'administration (ENA, whose closure President Macron announced in 2021), but I fluffed the interview. Instead I was cross-posted to Bonn, as second secretary responsible for the EEC. German had been my least favourite and least successful O-level; I got a B. However, I applied myself better at the second time of asking and passed the Advanced German exam.

During the four months I was in London between postings, I courted Olivia, who accepted my cack-handed proposal of marriage. The most important question of my life having been asked and answered, I left for Germany in November 1988.

The embassy on the B9 between Bonn and Friesdorf was over 400-strong: 100 UK-based staff and more than 300 colleagues on local contracts. Germany had the biggest and most successful economy in Europe, but much of the embassy's work focused on Cold War issues (commercial work was led by the consulate general up the road in Düsseldorf). As one of the four victorious allies, the UK had residual responsibilities in Berlin. The ambassador's main residence overlooked the Rhine, but he had an equally magnificent house in Grunewald in the old British Sector in Berlin, which he visited regularly.

In my first meeting with Pauline Neville-Jones[*] (minister, in other words, second-in-command at the embassy), I asked about the huge map of the Federal Republic on her

---

[*] Baroness Neville-Jones DCMG PC.

wall: 'Why do all such maps also show all of the German Democratic Republic?'

'Because of Berlin,' she replied, adding, 'and because West Germans have never given up hope of reuniting the country.'

At the end of 1988, this struck me as highly aspirational. But 1989 had other ideas. The excitement started in the East. Ever since its founding, the Federal Republic had encouraged citizens from the GDR to settle in the West. In 1961, the GDR reacted to the evident interest of its citizens in making that transition by building the Berlin Wall. However strenuously its authorities claimed its purpose was to keep undesirable Western elements out, it was plain to East Germans that its sole purpose was to keep them in.

By 1989, the attractions of life in a poor country with an oppressive government appealed to ever fewer East Germans. They were looking for new ways out. Few East Germans were allowed to travel to the West, but they were allowed to take holidays in Warsaw Pact countries and in 1989 Czechoslovakia and Hungary, with borders to Germany and Austria, had governments that were no longer prepared to ensure East German visitors returned home.

No one was directing, still less controlling, events. But, after Gorbachev's half-hearted attendance at ceremonies to celebrate forty years of the GDR, things unravelled quickly. The timing of the fall of the Berlin Wall was a surprise to everyone, but the abandonment of all efforts to prevent its people going to the FRG had been the unavoidable solution to the GDR's problems for months.

In the hope that something interesting would happen at the Communist Party spokesman's press conference, journalists flocked to East Berlin on 9 November 1989. Günther Schabowski outlined new travel regulations to an increasingly restless room. Journalists pressed him for a timetable. Improvising, Schabowski announced that implementation would be carried out 'unverzüglich' ('immediately'). That evening East Berliners went to crossing points in their thousands. Encountering guards without instructions apart from what they, like the massing crowds, had just heard Schabowski say, the people were allowed into West Berlin. The GDR died in one night. Its authorities knew the game was up but saw no advantage in publicising the fact.

It took the West, outside of the FRG, a curiously long time to work out the importance of 9 November. Senior figures were used to the status quo. Lots of players were slow or wrong, but I saw only one group at close quarters: the leadership of the British Embassy in Bonn.

Christopher Mallaby* was the ambassador, who had succeeded Julian Bullard in 1988. Earlier he had been minister in Bonn and first secretary in the UK's office in West Berlin. Pauline had also arrived in Bonn in 1988; it was her first posting to Germany. The head of chancery was Colin Budd,† another recent arrival.

Embassy leaders, especially Christopher, were well plugged into the government. They enjoyed access that all other embassies (apart from the Americans, French, and Soviets) envied. Their eminent sources were more than

---

* Sir Christopher Mallaby GCMG GCVO.
† Sir Colin Budd KCMG.

usually accessible and talkative in the autumn of 1989. They thought they were getting all the information they needed, indeed all the information there was to get. They were not. Why did they get it wrong?

Christopher and Pauline were the most experienced diplomats in the building. They had, it seemed, absolute faith in their own judgement. Their contacts were the most senior; they were not especially interested in entourages, because they were talking to the principals. And they could weave an apparently complete and compelling narrative from what they personally were told. But the most senior contacts were trying to influence embassy reporting to help themselves. Chancellor Kohl had identified Mrs Thatcher as the external player most likely to try to slow him down; he did not want Christopher's reporting to alarm her.

Christopher was always aware of what London, and particularly the prime minister, wanted to hear. Framing your message so it is better digested by your audience is fair enough. But the trimming and packaging must not disguise the substance of what your audience needs to understand. Mrs Thatcher's hostility to political change in Germany was clear and public from the beginning. Years later, Richard von Weizsäcker told me that he had visited London in 1990 in order to challenge and perhaps to change Mrs Thatcher's mind. He got nowhere. At the end of their meeting, the prime minister said, 'Mr President, I learned all I needed to know about Germany by 1942. Nothing that has happened since has caused me to change my mind.'

Not contradicting the prime minister's prejudices always seemed to have a higher priority than getting her to see the importance and inevitability of what was happening and the UK's limited ability to affect the direction or speed of events.

Personal ambition might explain some of Christopher's reluctance. Patrick was nearing retirement (at the time, this was the day before your sixtieth birthday) and Christopher wanted to succeed him as PUS. The prime minister signed off all permanent secretary appointments.

And their familiarity and comfort with the existing system meant they were not looking for its weaknesses. The UK had played a decisive role in constitutional arrangements in Germany since the Allied victory forty-four years earlier. The United States had always been closer to the UK than to Germany. Distrust and fear of the Soviet Union suffused all policy choices in Europe. They saw no reason to question their own assumptions.

Christopher and Pauline were daunting figures to challenge. They did not seek it and gave no hint that they would accept, still less welcome it. We all called Christopher 'Ambassador' (that of course was normal throughout the Service), but we also all stood whenever he swept into the room. His suite was cut off from the rest of the building. He engaged with his team mostly through his head of chancery.

Pauline was clever, quick, and intolerant. She was already the most senior woman in the Diplomatic Service, on her way to becoming the first female director general and political director. She thought the Office was wilfully sexist. And she was right. She was right most of the time. But the idea of compromise, or the notion that today's opponent might be tomorrow's ally on a different issue if handled with humour and respect, never seemed to occur to her.

But she was also perceptive, curious, and kind. She was the first person (apart from Olivia and me) to work out that my wife was pregnant with our first child. She could be generous, but often so late in the day that no amount of generosity could help her reputation.

Colin Budd stepped up. He was straightforward and approachable. He mediated between the ambassador and minister and everyone else. But he absorbed rather than dissipated pressure, which took a visible toll on him. In that era, the FCO had internal inspectors who travelled the world assessing the work of embassies and high commissions, to ensure the network was making the best use of its resources. At the end of Bonn's inspection, word went round the building that the chief inspector had told Christopher that 'fear was no longer an acceptable organising principle in an embassy'. Through Colin, we were informed that we no longer needed to stand when Christopher entered the room.

Christopher saw Helmut Kohl and Horst Teltschik regularly and reported their conversations meticulously. He made the points the prime minister wanted to be made and believed that British concerns were being factored into German planning, no matter the breathless ambition and timetable of Kohl's ten-point plan. He consistently underestimated German enthusiasm for unification and overestimated British influence on the outcome.

In January 1990, Christopher sent advice to London about the confederal solution. For the first time in writing he addressed the possibility of unification, saying events had developed to the point where some kind of unification might be imagined in five to ten years. I went to see Colin. I asked how he could allow the ambassador to send such rubbish when we both knew that unification would happen that year. 'Simon,' Colin replied, 'my achievement was dissuading him from saying that we could imagine unification in ten to fifteen years.'

Twenty years after he retired, Christopher published a memoir. The most unexpected part was the beginning, when as a boy he lost his father and became head of the family. Reading about his struggle, pride, and determination to protect those he loved made him a different man for me. But in Bonn he failed to get the best from his team; no one was able to relax in his presence. When he gave a public lecture about unification in Berlin in November 2011, he referred constantly to diary entries where he recorded insights that would have been validated if discussed more widely. Quoting his letters and telegrams (all publicly available by then) would not have impressed his audience: they were unimaginative, kowtowing to Thatcher, and wrong.

Other parts of the British system did better. The embassy in East Berlin had a better understanding of the collapse surrounding them. But the embassy in Bonn was the senior partner and listened to more carefully in London. Failings in Bonn were too great to be offset by excellent performance elsewhere. The most joyous events I witnessed – the fall of the Berlin Wall, the unification of Germany, and the end of the Cold War – were oddly disappointing professionally.

Looking back, most of my learning about leadership

was subconscious. At the time, I did not write down my dismay at poor examples of leadership. But I saw that effective leadership is not a one- or two-person job. I learned that, when crisis hits, you have to throw everything at its resolution, diverting resources deployed on less important tasks. When everything changes, imagination and curiosity are as important as experience and knowledge of what came before.

Most poor leaders I have come across have treated themselves seriously, encouraging (or at least accepting) deference from their colleagues. These characters can enjoy a long run of success before coming a cropper. In Germany, as ambassador, I came across a prime example, at the peak of his powers but with more in common with Louis XVI in 1788 than he realised.

Volkswagen is based at Wolfsburg in Lower Saxony. It is Exhibit A in Germany's *Wirtschaftswunder* ('economic miracle', also known as the Miracle on the Rhine). After the Second World War, a major in the British Army spotted the potential of the Third Reich's people's car. Instead of dismantling the production line (which the Soviets did to the car companies located in their zone of occupation), he directed its reconstruction. Ivan Hirst set the company back on its feet; Volkswagen was grateful enough to supply him with a new car from their range every year until his death in 2000.

In the twenty-first century, Volkswagen's factory continues to dominate Wolfsburg's skyline. It takes the Berlin to Hanover train, pulling out of Wolfsburg railway station, a full minute to pass its 2-kilometre length. The chairman has his office in the tallest building. When I called on him in 2013, petitioners were lining up in an antechamber, which was decorated like the lair of a Bond villain. After a few minutes, Herr Winterkorn burst from his inner sanctum, escorting the minister of economics. Herr Altmaier looked shell-shocked but managed to sign the visitors' book and smile for a photograph.

Once the minister had been bundled off the penthouse floor, Herr Winterkorn turned to me. He was solicitous as he showed me and my first secretary into his conference room. He was also disconcertingly tactile, placing his hand on my arm throughout our interview. He talked incessantly. Everything about the set-up screamed, 'I'm in charge. We'll get along just fine if you remember that.' He looked as if he would deal with the bringer of bad news as temperately as a Roman emperor.

Less than two years later, Herr Winterkorn resigned in disgrace when it was revealed that Volkswagen, under his stewardship, had systematically cheated in emissions' tests for its diesel engines. Germany's highest-paid business-man clattered to the ground with no one expressing regret. I met Herr Winterkorn only once. I include him to show that imperious leadership quickly makes itself apparent. His example also neatly proves the point that, although the style can work for a time (sometimes a long time), in the end it cannot endure, and it departs unmourned.

As distressing to work for as an imperious leader is a weak one. In 2000, I was working in Riyadh when the kingdom suffered its first significant domestic terrorist attack since Juhayman al-Otaibi stormed the Great Mosque in Mecca in 1979. British expatriates who ran bars in residential compounds were targeted. One man was killed in the first attack. The Saudi authorities jumped to the conclusion that other Britons were responsible, engaged in turf wars to dominate the profitable and illegal alcohol trade. The Britons who were arrested protested their innocence: their business was established and relied on complete discretion – drawing themselves to the authorities' attention would destroy their business model. After lengthy detention in solitary confinement, the Saudis persuaded them to make full, filmed confessions.

Having settled their story, the Saudis sought supporting evidence. One hole in the narrative was the sourcing of the explosives used in the home-made bombs. The minister for the interior summoned the ambassador, Derek Plumbly,* to discuss possibilities. I accompanied him but was kept in an antechamber with officials. They took a particular interest in me, inviting me to write out my name. I saw no harm in complying.

Not long afterwards, the minister summoned Derek without me. In that meeting they said that the detainees had implicated me, claiming that they had operated under my instructions, using explosives that I had given them at the British Embassy, explosives that I had smuggled into the country in the diplomatic bag. They accused me of conspiracy to murder. Derek wrung his hands.

The drama unfolded in the final weeks of my posting. Robin Cook had already offered me the job of principal

---

* Sir Derek Plumbly KCMG.

private secretary; I was due to take over immediately after the general election, expected in May 2001. The Office, through John Kerr (PUS at the time), expressed its full confidence. My next job was confirmed. John sent me a personal message, in a style unmistakably his own. It meant a lot.

Derek continued to wring his hands. Throughout he acted as if his main concern was the problem (of which I had become a central part) of maintaining the smooth relationship of the UK with Saudi Arabia and his successful mission as ambassador. On the eve of my departure, I set out my assessment of the shortcomings of his approach in writing. For the first time since his arrival in Riyadh, he called on me at home.

We had a blazing row, the only time I have lost my temper at work, complete with raised voices. I reminded Derek that, instead of demanding evidence, he had suggested I submit myself for questioning by the Metropolitan Police. Two Met detectives conducted a long, bewildering recorded session in the basement of the Old Admiralty Building. Eventually, with the help of Olivia's comprehensive family diaries, I was able to prove to their satisfaction a series of negatives: that I had never met any of the prisoners; that I had never had any contact with them, either direct or indirect; that I had nothing whatsoever to do with murder or terrorism.

In our row, I pointed out that we (that is, the British government) knew that the version of events relayed by the Saudis was nonsense. We were entitled to conclude various things from that knowledge. We were entitled to ask why the prisoners were spouting nonsense and to conclude that they were confessing under pressure. More than that, the prisoners might reasonably hope that, knowing the version of events attributed to them was fabricated, we might apply pressure to the Saudis. We did none of those things. At no point, as far as I could see, did Derek challenge the Saudis. Instead he judged it prudent to engage on their terms; by not antagonising the Saudis, he hoped to secure the release of British prisoners.

The investigation persisted for a time but petered out. One emerging problem for the Saudi version was the fact that bombs continued to go off, even after all the alleged culprits were incarcerated. Eventually the veteran Saudi foreign minister called on the new foreign secretary (Jack Straw had succeeded Robin the day after the delayed election in June) and said that 'no aspersion' should attach to any British official. As the new PPS, I was sitting at the dining table in 1 Carlton Gardens.

That was that for me. The situation of the nine Britons, imprisoned in Saudi gaols, was far, far worse. They languished there until June 2003, when Crown Prince Abdullah agreed their release after meeting Prime Minister Blair in the margins of the Evian G8 Summit.

I got through with some help from John Kerr and masses of help from Olivia. I learned that, if the facts demand it, you must back your team, no matter the consequences for the official agenda. Leaders without a team that trusts them are solitary in a self-harming way: inadequately knowledge-able, thinly stretched chancers.

3

Leadership Done Well

In 1990, Olivia and I were on holiday in the Black Forest when I received a phone call from Colin Budd: 'The foreign secretary [Douglas Hurd] wants to see you next week. Don't get too excited – he doesn't want you to be private secretary. But he does want to interview you to be his speech-writer.' I got the job. Mrs Hurd intervened, apparently, to make the start date more humane. Olivia was heavily pregnant with our first child. Douglas accepted Judy's ruling that the confinement should be in Germany and that a baby could not move countries for two or three weeks. Our eldest son was born in mid-August. My parents-in-law collected him and Olivia by car at the beginning of September. I packed up the house and followed by air a couple of days later.

A few weeks afterwards, Douglas attended the celebrations at the German Embassy to mark Unification Day. He gave a speech. His audience was moved to tears. As his speech-writer, I was asked for the text. There was none; he had spoken off-the-cuff. Someone found an amateur video clip but the transcript was gobbledygook. I learned that, as someone who had been a speech-writer himself (for Edward Heath), Douglas needed minimal help with some of his most important speeches, and that the spoken word is fundamentally different from the written word. Repetition and deviation, which are not tolerated in writing, can add impact when speaking. And audiences pay more attention to a speaker who speaks without a text, who looks them in the eye and can adjust pacing, length, and content in response to that audience. It was going to be tough working for someone who had worked all that out decades ago.

In those days, the speech-writer was a member of Policy Planning Staff. My head of department was Robert Cooper,* setting a standard for policy challenge which none of his successors has quite matched. The assistant head was Jonathan Powell (Downing Street chief of staff, 1997–2007) and one of the two other first secretary desk officers was Simon Fraser (PUS, 2010–15).† It was the moment in my career in which I was working with the highest concentration of future senior leaders.

Robert always appeared to have time and never showed stress. He once told me that that was partly because he never felt he was really working. He read voraciously for pleasure, but it always turned out that his reading was relevant to his work. From Robert I learned the difference between strategy and policy: strategy was overarching, durable, and capable of being expressed pithily. My favourite, heard first from Robert, was Lord Ismay's justification, from Western Europe's point of view, for NATO: 'To keep the Soviet Union out, the Americans in, and the Germans

---

* Sir Robert Cooper KCMG MVO.
† Sir Simon Fraser GCMG.

down.' (NATO has been in existential trouble since the Soviet Union dissolved and a reunited Germany definitively took its place in the West at the beginning of the 1990s; Vladimir Putin came to its rescue in 2022.)

Jonathan felt policy was an undervalued and underworked idea compared to strategy: policy was what you did, sometimes amounting to no more than what you said, and what you hoped for, when confronted by any issue. In any given situation, it was better to have a policy than not, but the policy had neither to be elaborate nor long-term: the key was that it should be fit for the moment to defend and promote the UK interest.

Jonathan also introduced me to the most serviceable explanation for why any country has a foreign policy. Its aim, always, was to promote peace, prosperity, and prestige. Every national security strategy has been based on these three aims, even if subdivided or dressed up in grander language.

The Policy Planning Staff in those days reported direct to the foreign secretary. Douglas Hurd was the best-prepared foreign secretary in my time in the Foreign Office. After fourteen years in the Diplomatic Service, including postings to Beijing and Rome, he resigned to become Edward Heath's private secretary in 1966. He was elected MP for Mid Oxfordshire in 1974 and became minister of state for Europe at the FCO when the Conservatives returned to power in 1979. He served as junior minister at the Home Office for one year after the election in 1983, before joining the cabinet as secretary of state for Northern Ireland. After one year there and four years as home secretary, he returned to the FCO as foreign secretary in 1989. He was the only foreign secretary I saw able to conduct a competent TV interview in French.

There are no golden eras, just golden and selective memories of periods in the past which others do not have the knowledge to challenge. But the early 1990s was a good era for the process of foreign policymaking. The FCO had a chief who was sympathetic to the Office and who was respected, both in Downing Street and in international meetings. The ministerial team worked harmoniously and uncompetitively with their chief and many served long periods (Lynda Chalker racked up eight years as minister for Africa and international development). John Major liked and listened to Douglas, and he knew something about the FCO and its leading personalities from his three-month stint as foreign secretary. Douglas worked easily with his three PUSs.

Because I was a junior officer with relatively frequent access to the foreign secretary, the training department (responsible for induction) asked me to brief new entrants about working at the heart of the FCO. I did my stuff and, in answer to a question, said something like Douglas Hurd was brilliant but a bit distant. Some time later I heard that this cohort of new entrants had been vastly entertained by some pipsqueak in their induction briefing laying into Douglas as a dreadful boss – 'Just who does he think he is?' Years later I discovered that I was the guilty briefer, the audience having heard a harsher assessment than I had intended.

Patrick was coming to the end of his tenure when Douglas arrived. In the 1990s, procedures to choose top civil servants were mysterious to everyone who was not directly involved in taking the final decision. Like the Vatican, senior contenders spent years eyeing each other up, weighing who was *papabile*. The choice was always internal and often appeared inevitable after it was announced. In 1990, David Hannay looked like the obvious candidate.

His name was submitted to 10 Downing Street. Prime ministers have always signed off permanent secretary appointments – only their directive role is of recent vintage. But in 1990 everyone accepted Margaret Thatcher's veto power. According to her foreign affairs private secretary, she reacted with dismay when told of the plan: 'Oh, no! David is like a pneumatic drill: all very well in its place but you wouldn't want one next door.'

David Hannay and David Gillmore* swapped proposed jobs: Hannay went as permanent representative to the United Nations in New York and Gillmore became PUS. The political level imposed a better deployment of talent than the Service would have managed by itself. In New York, Hannay deftly orchestrated the succession of Russia to the Soviet Union's permanent seat on the Security Council before anyone had spotted there might be alternative futures, and he helped launch Responsibility to Protect as a governing principle of the UN's work. In London, Gillmore presided over an expansion of the diplomatic network as a score of new countries established themselves in the wake of the dissolution of the Soviet Union, Yugoslavia, and Czechoslovakia.

---

* Lord Gillmore of Thamesfield GCMG.

After I had been writing speeches for Douglas for two years, he almost recruited me as a private secretary. The interview went well but, as we were both on our feet and I was heading for the door, he asked about my family. I said that Olivia and I feared our two-bedroom flat would be a bit of a squeeze, now Olivia was expecting our second child. Douglas stopped in his tracks and said (something like): 'I know more than you about what work patterns suit a young family.'

Instead, David Gillmore recruited me as his private secretary. He was a wonderful man, actively kind to everyone, patient, funny, inexhaustible, and unstuffy. I have few specific memories of that time, but the impression those years left was of a happy glow. I remember he took time to help younger colleagues in difficulty. I remember the care he took chairing the No 1 Board (the senior appointments board). He was unhappy with only one decision, the only time when he disagreed with the majority of the board. He predicted disaster, which, within eighteen months, would indeed befall the colleague sent to a job David argued was wrong for him.

I remember going into his office one afternoon just after he had taken a call on his private line. In the outer office we knew when he was on the phone because a light lit up on our own phones. Private calls were rare. David was standing at his desk, looking down, when I walked in. 'My mother just died,' he said bleakly, feeling what those words meant for the first time. I mumbled something about him going home to see his family and I felt a pang that I did not have a clue how to help a friend in distress.

David served for only three years as PUS. Because Douglas was still foreign secretary, he played the decisive role in choosing his successor. He wanted someone with experience of the FCO Board, as a head of mission and, if possible, knowledge of Number 10 and/or the Cabinet Office. Discussion quickly focused on two candidates.

At this point, Rachel Johnson invited me to lunch. We had worked together in Policy Planning Staff when I was speech-writer and she was a secondee from the *Financial Times*. She was fascinated by the succession stakes, and I was happy to assess the strengths and weaknesses of the field for her. I was less happy when an account of our conversation appeared later in the week in the *FT*. No one ever asked whether I was the source, probably because they assumed that, had I been, I would have mentioned the name of the favourite to win. I had, but Rachel forgot to include John Coles* in her piece. I learned that journalists are not obliged to set out the terms of any conversation; those they talk to, are.

John Coles succeeded David as PUS in August 1994. I worked for him for less than a year before being posted to Washington – then, as now, our largest and most prestig-ious embassy. The ambassador was Robin Renwick,† clearly enjoying the final days of his mission and his diplomatic career. He was succeeded by John Kerr, the FCO's leading EU expert, doing something different on his way to becom-ing PUS. When, as expected, he in turn succeeded John

---

* Sir John Coles GCMG.
† Lord Renwick of Clifton KCMG.

Coles, he was replaced by Christopher Meyer,* plucked out of Bonn after just seven months. The Germans were not thrilled by this incontrovertible proof of the hierarchy of UK overseas interests. But Christopher did remain in Germany long enough to meet, woo, and wed his second wife, Catherine, who was introduced to Washington colleagues on Christopher's first day in the job, meeting us even before she had met his sons.

My three Washington ambassadors were heavily contrasting characters who looked unnervingly similar (pencil-thin and grey, although Christopher wore red socks). They ran the UK's most important diplomatic mission and lived in the only Lutyens mansion in North America. For people who had arrived at the top, they spent a lot of time worrying about their access, in particular to important meetings between the leaders of the American and British systems. As head of chancery, John had wheedled his way into Camp David meetings from which protocol on both sides had striven to exclude him. But an ambassador could not sit on the floor or under a table to secure admission.

Negotiations about attendance were never straightforward and not always successful from the ambassador's point of view. The oddest argument wheeled out by the Americans to exclude them was their desire to exclude their own ambassador from meetings. In protocol terms, ambassadors were paired: you could not have one without having the other. Even though all American ambassadors to London (with the single exception of Ray Seitz at the

---

* Sir Christopher Meyer KCMG.

end of the 1980s) were political appointees, it seemed that their relations with and reputations in the Oval Office were sometimes poor.

One way the British system invested in the relationship with the US was to have a first secretary devoted to following American politics. The highlight of this four-year posting was the presidential election. US presidents appoint over 3,000 officials, most in Washington, but also every US ambassador. Many of these jobs are filled by people who worked and raised funds for the president when they were a candidate on the campaign trail. Once appointed, these people were often too busy or grand to deal with embassies in DC, but they were happy to keep in touch with a first secretary they met in a diner in Des Moines or in the margins of a rally in Manchester, New Hampshire.

My predecessor in this job hit pay dirt. In 1991, President George H. W. Bush was riding high in the polls on the back of victory in the Gulf War. Saddam Hussein had been expelled from Kuwait, and Bush was enjoying an 89% approval rating. His re-election seemed assured. That being the case, there was no point in a British first secretary trailing along behind his triumphal procession. Instead, Jonathan Powell looked at the thin field of democratic challengers and alighted on Governor Clinton. Interest was so low in the early stages of the Clinton campaign (including a third-place finish in Iowa and second place in New Hampshire) that Clinton's team made space and time for Jonathan. When the gamble paid off and Clinton was elected president, the benefits were personal to Jonathan as well as general to the British system. Tony Blair, newly installed as leader of the Labour Party in 1994, made an early visit to Washington to learn from the 'war room' campaign techniques pioneered by Clinton and his team. Jonathan guided Blair authoritatively through new Washington. Soon afterwards he left the FCO to become Blair's chief of staff.

My presidential election was more humdrum. I got to know many of the people circling Senator Dole but not even Mrs Dole was surprised when he lost. Blair's election as prime minister followed hot on the heels of Clinton's second victory. Clinton's second term was overshadowed by the Lewinsky scandal, which broke over the Administration in January 1998. At the time we were in the final stages of preparing Blair's visit to the US at the beginning of February. After a brief discussion among officials about the optics of standing by (and therefore implicitly supporting) the president in his hour of need, the PM decided to proceed. The gesture (and implied support) was appreciated by Clinton, who took a more active interest in Blair's Third Way. Leaders in trouble notice who stick around among those who do not need to and are grateful, even when a cool-headed analysis might have concluded that their difficulty was likely to be temporary.

My main memory of Blair personally from our first encounter was how young he looked. Although forty-four, he looked like a teenager. I feared a fresh face would not be taken seriously. But leaders have often risen to power when young. From Alexander the Great (weeping for lack of new worlds to conquer at thirty) to Augustus (first Roman emperor at thirty-five) to Charlemagne (king of the Franks at twenty-one) to Napoleon (self-crowned emperor at thirty-three) leaders have often risen fast and burned out quickly. They are defined by their success rather than their youth. Americans respected and responded to Blair's power. Of course, young leaders in the past had usually been schooled in leadership from childhood (it must help to have Aristotle as a teacher); they were either always expected to become leader or had displayed precocious military prowess. Blair's rise to the top was neither planned by others nor preceded by a string of battle honours: he benefited from chance (the untimely death of John Smith), the exhaustion of his opponents (in government for eighteen years), and an electorate looking for change.

Blair's visit took place in my final year in Washington. I was among the last FCO cohort to be promoted to counsellor/SMS1 without needing to pass an Assessment and Development Centre. Andrew Green was looking for a new deputy in Riyadh and wanted me. The process ran smoothly, and I arrived back in Riyadh in December 1998.

4

Leading for the First Time

Until I arrived in Riyadh the second time, in the first sixteen years of my career, I had never had to line manage more than two people at a time; until Bonn (six years in) I had managed no one at all. Overnight, I found myself second-in-command in an embassy of over 120 people, with the largest line management responsibility. Sometimes you either sink or swim.

After my first year as deputy head of mission, I said that in the job I had had to deal with everything apart from murder and incest. By the time I left, sixteen months later, the list of excluded issues was reduced to one. DHMs know most about what is happening in the mission. They are an ambassador's key adviser and occasional replacement. Ambassadors necessarily face outwards, to the countries to which they are accredited and to London. DHMs ensure that the mission functions smoothly internally. For health reasons, Andrew was absent from Saudi Arabia for much of the time I was his deputy. His departure was followed by a long interregnum before Derek Plumbly's arrival. So, I had a long stint as chargé d'affaires, giving me a chance to lead an overseas team. Acting as chargé is the best training for being an ambassador later: everything is in your hands, temporarily; you swing on the flying trapeze for the first time with the safety net of your chief's imminent return to give you confidence.

You have to know everyone in your team if you are going to get the best out of them. The security guards, receptionists, and registry clerks were as important to making my working life enjoyable and the embassy productive as the counsellors and first secretaries. President Kennedy's visit to NASA at Cape Canaveral in 1963 illustrates the point. Spotting a man somewhat removed from the receiving line, the president walked over, introduced himself and asked the man what he was doing. The janitor replied: 'I'm helping to put a man on the moon.' Precisely.

I tried to learn everyone's name and discovered it is difficult, especially when your team is big or constantly changing. But it is worth the effort. Categories with a title that shows respect are a help to an overcrowded memory: ambassadors never mind being called 'Excellency', so I remembered the names only of ambassadors who were friends. King Hussein used to call all male foreign guests 'Sir', which his guests found charming and which, no doubt, spared the king much mental effort.

Leaders take decisions. And leaders in the field must interpret instructions from the centre. When Andrew left, one of the biggest decisions left to me was how the embassy should prepare for the millennium bug (Y2K). In 1998 and 1999 much of the world convinced itself that computers would turn themselves off at midnight on 1 January 2000. Organisations prepared expensively to meet the challenge.

Patrick, a non-executive director on the board, told me that BP had spent £1.5 billion on new computing capacity.

Throughout 1999 I received no answer to two questions: why would computers, recognising zero as a digit when placed second in a number, and recognising other double repeated digits as numbers, decide 'oo' was not a number and turn off as a consequence of that decision? And surely someone, fearing a global meltdown on 1 January, had built a computer and programmed it as if it were, say, six months earlier, so we would have evidence in advance of what happened when a computer hit 'oo'?

Meanwhile, other embassies spent lavishly on their preparations. The Americans installed new generators in all their staff housing. In the British embassy, we spent SR40 (about £8) on two jerrycans in order to have more fuel on the compound. The Saudis had told us that the way their infrastructure was most likely to be affected was petrol pumps ceasing to operate until they could be reset. And then we waited. I went camping on 31 December. The moon having set early, the desert sky was as full of stars as I can remember.

In the morning, precisely nothing happened. Y2K turned out not to be a thing. Countries that had spent nothing on preparations (Cuba) suffered as few problems as G8 countries that had spent billions. My team noticed, but no one else gave me any credit. I felt my situation was similar to, but crucially different from, the boy in Hans Christian Andersen's story 'The Emperor's New Clothes'. Those peddling the Y2K problem were analogous to the weavers of invisible thread. But the computer makers made money out of everyone they'd persuaded that Y2K was a problem: governments, companies, and individuals bought their wares, not simply one gullible despot. When so many had fallen for the weavers' warnings, they were able successfully to remain silent rather than face up to the fact that they had been duped. I saw that there was nothing to be gained by saying, 'I told you so', but I was left with the uneasy feeling that, had I been wrong, the majority in the right would not have been so understanding. We are incentivised to join the consensus, even when we judge that the consensus is making a mistake.

A few years later I discussed Y2K with the man who had been the FCO's chief information officer at the time. He conceded that we had acted on the gloomiest predictions of people who had stood to make substantial money out of others acting on those gloomy predictions. But, he added, the global investment had proved worthwhile in the medium term. When American Airlines Flight 11 and United Airlines Flight 175 took out the Twin Towers in Lower Manhattan on Tuesday 11 September the following year, back-up computing capacity installed in New Jersey in 1999 took the strain. Because of New York's preparations for Y2K, the world's leading financial centre was able to carry on, despite the collapse of the Twin Towers.

I was noisier about one other failure of judgment at head office. In 1999 the British government decided to back the Football Association's bid for the 2006 FIFA World Cup. In 2000 the most financially consequential decision in sport was taken by the twenty-four men and one woman who made up FIFA's Executive Committee. The bid team was led by Tony Banks, who had stepped down as minister of sport in order to devote himself full-time to the bid. He toured the world with Geoff Hurst, the first man to score a hat-trick in a football World Cup final.

With such a small electorate, the lobbying task was straightforward. Around the world, embassies with an Executive Committee member living on their patch had to get to know them. I flew to Dammam to meet Abdullah al-Dabal, who had been a member of the Executive Committee since 1986.

Over the course of six months and a handful of meetings, I got to know Abdullah well enough for him, as he put it, 'to put me out of my misery'. He explained to me exactly how the vote for who would host the 2006 World Cup would unfold and why: 'It's very simple, Simon: Germany will win. Eight years ago, Bert Millichip did a deal with Franz Beckenbauer: Germany would support England's bid for UEFA Euro 1996 in exchange for English support for Germany to host the World Cup in 2006.

'In the Executive Committee, the England bid is seen as bad form. I know the FA disputes the existence of a deal; they say either that Bert wasn't authorised to make a deal or he wasn't in his right mind and Franz over-interpreted the promise of an ailing man. But the point, Simon, is that everyone on the Executive Committee – I stress, everyone – believes there was a deal. Franz Beckenbauer is one of us; he's respected by all of us; even we call him the Kaiser. And he has told us solemnly that there was a deal. Your people have to understand, first, that we believe him, and, second, that there's precisely zero chance that you'll dissuade us from continuing to believe him.'

I reported Abdullah's analysis. I put my advice in a tel-
eletter. I recommended that we fold our tent with good
grace, back Germany, and focus on securing the competition after the turn of Africa and Latin America. Before
email, teleletters were the best way to get a message quickly
to a small audience. When inviting anyone to reconsider,
you give yourself your best chance by making as few others
as possible know your advice. But my advice made precisely
no impression in London. And, when the Executive Committee gathered in Zurich in July 2000, the vote proceeded
exactly as Abdullah had predicted: Germany won the right
to host the FIFA World Cup in 2006.

From the start, leadership feels lonely, as if loneliness is
an inevitable ingredient. To make it less lonely, I tried to
draw my team closer. If they knew me and my motivations
better, they would be happier to be led by me (I reasoned).
Still, as a leader of a large team for the first time, I did
not open up much. Looking back, I took care not to allow
the wrong impression to take root. People, including other
British diplomats, generally assume a lot about British diplomats. But, first time around, I found it hard to share what
I really cared about, to the extent that I considered sharing
it. Being open about myself was something I gradually realised was important. In the light of that realisation, I find
my time as DHM wanting. It was not enough to be unapologetic about being a grammar school Roman Catholic
from Salford.

In Riyadh, I was able to develop my second strategy
for coping with the loneliness of leadership: confiding in
Olivia. About everything. Well, about nearly everything,

keeping personnel issues confidential. I needed to talk things through with someone whose observations would surprise and challenge me, while always supporting me. I am as certain of Olivia's discretion as I can be of anything in the world.

Leading for the first time was a shock. The training offered in preparation was rudimentary: essential stuff about your dealing with the money and checking the account, and optional stuff about crisis management, consular work, and dealing with the press (all this optional training has become obligatory in the last twenty years). I had only six weeks between leaving Washington and arriving in Riyadh, so my options were few. But formal training was largely beside the point. Eighteen years of watching others do it well and do it badly was my main guide.

An old childhood fable floated to the surface of my memory. The story of the sun and the wind was a favourite of Mr Kirrane, my teacher in Junior 3. One day, the wind was arguing with the sun about which was more powerful. Unable to resolve their row, the wind suggested a practical test. He pointed out a man walking down a street dressed in an overcoat. He said that whichever was able to force the man to take off his coat would be crowned the winner. The sun accepted the bet. The fierce wind went first, blowing with all his might. He stripped leaves from the trees and sent everything that was not tied down sailing through the air. But the man clutched his coat around him tighter; the harder the wind blew, the tighter the man's grip. After a time, the wind gave up, spent. The sun peeped from behind the clouds that the wind had sent scudding across the sky.

She warmed the devastated scene. The man turned down the collar flap on his coat and turned his face towards the sun. The gentle sun slowly increased her warmth. Before long, the man had unbuttoned his coat. As the wind looked on in dismay, the man slipped off his coat and draped it over his shoulder. The sun won the bet.

A story first heard as a nine-year-old contained a truth that had eluded my worst leaders: kindness, rather than ferocity, is most likely to get the best out of your team. Obvious. Easy to say. Most leaders would agree when considering the point in theory. But the trick was to apply the lesson consistently in practice: when time was short, when someone's first effort had fallen short in your opinion, or when the way ahead was clear to you but resisted by your team. Patrick, Julian, and David always had five minutes, no matter how hectic their day, and their teams always knew they had five minutes; it was not a discovery made in extremis. I tried to lead like them.

5

Leadership at the Centre

When John Kerr visited Riyadh in the winter of 2001, he took me aside: 'I hear you're interested in being the next principal private secretary to the foreign secretary. I think you should have an interview.' Until twenty years ago, interviews were rare, generally only for private office jobs; other roles were decided by boards, guided by the Personnel/HR department. After passing my Final Selection Board, I had only ten interviews for particular jobs in the FCO or Cabinet Office in the following thirty-eight years.

Robin Cook interviewed me in February 2001, three months before a general election was expected. The timing was unusual, but the incumbent PPS (Sherard Cowper-Coles) needed to start preparing for his next job as ambassador to Israel and John Kerr, who endured a notoriously scratchy relationship with Cook, wanted to signal his confidence in Cook's reappointment to the Foreign Office by allowing him to choose the next PPS before the election.

Robin saw me in his huge red and gilt office at the corner of the first floor of Downing Street West. The office had been restored since Douglas's days as foreign secretary. The leather-bound volumes of state papers in the bookcase had been replaced by artefacts showcasing modern Britain, including a wind-up radio and a Raspberry Pi computer. The painting of a nineteenth-century Nepalese prince, which had hung over the fireplace, had been reclaimed by the British Museum and replaced by a less imperial image, prominently featuring a box of cornflakes.* I answered Robin's questions. Not for the last time, I felt I would be disappointed not to get the job on the back of an interview when the interviewer did not seem particularly engaged. At the end he asked me if I had any questions. I did not. And I did not invent one under pressure. So I left feeling I had let myself down.

I flew back to Riyadh the same day. More or less as soon as I landed, Sherard phoned to tell me that I had got the job. I immediately began planning my departure, at the same time trying to relax and pack in family time, knowing that the next two years would be frenetic. Like a hedgehog bulking up on insects and snails before hibernation, I tried to store happy, soothing memories to be drawn on later. The effort was probably doomed to fail, human well-being having little in common with a hedgehog's digestive system, even before the Ministry of the Interior's effort to link me to Saudi domestic terrorism knocked it completely off course.

The date for packers to collect our heavy baggage was already in the diary when foot and mouth disease broke out

---

* John Bratby's *Window, Dartmouth Row, Blackheath*. One year later, an FCO historian told me that the huge gilt-framed mirror designed for the space above the fireplace was hanging in a ground floor room elsewhere in the building. Jack Straw had it restored to its original position. It is still there.

on a farm in Heddon-on-the-Wall at the end of February. We left in early May, even though the general election had been postponed until 7 June. We went house-hunting while we waited.

As expected, Labour comfortably maintained their majority in the House of Commons. But the cabinet reshuffle that followed on 8 June was not quite as expected. Robin Cook went into 10 Downing Street in the morning but did not emerge until late in the evening. Sherard was in touch from time to time, sounding decreasingly confident of Robin's return.

Nobody in British politics is as powerful as a re-elected prime minister the morning after an election victory. Tony Blair chose to use that moment of maximum leverage to displace his foreign secretary. Robin had little option but to accept the demotion to leader of the House of Commons. But he argued through the afternoon about the grace-and-favour accommodation that had been his as foreign secretary. He wanted to keep both the flat at the top of 1 Carlton Gardens and Chevening House.

Jack Straw had expected to become transport secretary (he had worked out how to get Heathrow a third runway) but knew that nothing was confirmed until the audience with the prime minister. He waited for the summons to Number 10. By the early afternoon, his impatience got the better of him and he went, uninvited, to Downing Street. Number 10 has numerous antechambers and a prime minister has as many flunkies who can distract or divert a petitioner. Jack was kept at bay until Blair was ready to see him. He was flabbergasted. Later he told me that he had always hoped one day to serve as foreign secretary but not for a few more years. With an oath, he accepted the offer.

The tussle over accommodation was solved quickly. The Straws had no intention of leaving their home in Oval, already elaborately adapted to the security needs of a home secretary; the Cooks could keep Carlton Gardens. But the Straws took Chevening House, traditionally used by foreign secretaries to entertain (and impress) overseas visitors. The bargain struck, Jack went home to celebrate with his family.

The next morning I was summoned to meet the new foreign secretary, in effect to be reinterviewed for the PPS job. I waited in an outer office with one of Robin's special advisers, also hoping to stay on with the new boss. Michael Williams was a human rights and UN specialist with no interest in following Robin to the lord president's office. Our nerves were unfounded. Later, Jack told me that his celebrations had been so thorough that, as long as I was an English-speaking humanoid, the job was mine.

In the summer of 2001, Macedonia was the main foreign policy preoccupation. At lunchtime on 11 September, Jack was about to meet Geoff Hoon, the defence secretary, in his office to discuss some aspect of British involvement in the Balkans when American Airlines Flight 11 hit the North Tower of the World Trade Center in Manhattan. The meeting proceeded while officials tried to find out exactly what had happened. A quarter of an hour later, my deputy, Mark Sedwill,* burst into the foreign secretary's office and

---

* Lord Sedwill GCMG.

said the South Tower had also been hit. In an instant the world changed.

The aftermath of 9/11 dominated Jack's time as foreign secretary. Attention focussed first on Afghanistan. The refusal of Taliban leader Mullah Mohammad Omar immediately to hand over Osama bin Laden, who boasted of planning the 9/11 attacks from the caves of Tora Bora where he had taken refuge after his expulsion from Sudan, led to an American-led attack on Afghanistan. The mission creep that followed the fall of the Taliban government was a problem for Jack's successors. For as long as he was foreign secretary, the attack on Afghanistan was the most easily explained and widely understood reaction to 9/11: the US and its allies would hold responsible those who gave refuge to those who attacked them as well as the attackers themselves.

The problems in Afghanistan started as soon as the first objective was achieved and the Taliban regime was overthrown. Having achieved the first objective with apparent ease, the international community expanded the mission. In the decade after the end of the Cold War, the US thought there was nothing in world politics it could not do. To transform a society, by most measures the US and its partners cared about one of the least developed societies in the world, seemed noble and achievable.

Those on the ground quickly worked out that, although the Taliban had been displaced, they had not been defeated. Their networks and their mindset remained in place, biding their time. The international coalition could keep its puppet government in place only as long as it was prepared to remain in force on the ground. And remaining in force was expensive and created new problems inside Afghanistan. Every time coalition forces killed a local, it magnified its problems.

The puppets – Hamid Karzai and then Ashraf Ghani – had little local legitimacy and were not up to the job. They were supported to the hilt, initially. But nearly all the international effort was military: the US spent $3 trillion, with barely $3 billion spent on development over twenty years. The puppets, and their opponents, worked out that they would remain in place only as long as military support continued, because the government was not becoming more capable. Quite the contrary: the government was becoming ever more corrupt; such development assistance as was distributed was more likely to line the pockets of government ministers and officials than help ordinary Afghans.

Despite the advice of people on the ground – notably Sherard Cowper-Coles – ministers reaffirmed, again and again, their vaulting ambition to transform the country. Watershed moments that might have allowed a scaling back were allowed to pass. So, the change of Administration from Bush to Obama (and Brown to Cameron) and the killing of Osama bin Laden did not change policy.

Without ever being acknowledged, the following key facts were set in concrete before Bush left office: Afghanistan could absorb all the resource the coalition was prepared to devote to it without changing fundamentally; most Afghans were not reconciled to the outside presence; and, as soon as that presence left, Afghans would settle their governance in the way that suited them rather than outsiders.

At some level, the key governments recognised this by postponing difficult decisions on drawdown and withdrawal. It always seems easier to postpone the disagreeable – in this case the admission that, after initial success, the mission had grown without thought of how or when or in what necessarily sub-optimal conditions it would end.

When the International Security Assistance Force wound up its operations at the end of 2014, the endgame began inexorably to play itself out. Afghanistan was not like Germany, Japan, or Korea, where the local population recognised the value of an outside force staying on, long after formal conflict had ended, in order to guarantee peace and ensure no recurrence of fighting. The Afghans who counted were explicit that outsiders were there under sufferance. Their presence was tolerated so long as it was small, time-limited, and declining. President Trump's deal and President Biden's withdrawal, silently but effectively, acknowledged that fact.

In 2002 that denouement (although already locked in) lay in the distant future. Instead, attention shifted increasingly to Iraq. Looking back, the key decisions were taken early in the crisis with few people involved. The main decision makers were in Washington, in the immediate vicinity of President George W. Bush. Vice President Cheney and Defense Secretary Rumsfeld were the president's main advisers; they did not conceal that, for them, Saddam Hussein was unfinished business from the Administration of President George H. W. Bush.

In London, the main decision maker was Tony Blair. His primary advisers were Jonathan Powell and Alastair

Campbell, his director of communications. Early on, President Bush explained his thinking to the PM, dwelling on the continuing danger Saddam Hussein and Iraqi weapons of mass destruction (WMD) posed to the international community, his determination to remove them once and for all, and his view that this would be the acid test for US relations with all its partners. Blair left Bush with the impression that the UK would stand by the US, no matter what. The centrality of the strategic relationship with the United States (particularly its defence and intelligence elements) and his personal relationship with the president shaped the PM's decisions throughout.

Jack was often in the room but never inside the PM's head. He continuously tested the PM's thinking, to the point where the challenge became irritating to the PM's inner circle. He asked whether Iraq possessed the WMD programme of most concern, and was disconcerted when initial research suggested that Libyan, Iranian, and North Korean programmes (all with nuclear components, which Iraq no longer had) were potentially a greater threat. Subsequent work, focusing on intent as much as capability, restored Iraq to the status of country of most concern.

With more frequent contact with a broader range of foreign leaders, Jack was also more conscious than the PM of the importance of the process preceding any conflict. Saddam had to be given a ladder to climb down. The international community needed to see that every effort had been made to achieve the desired result of depriving Iraq of its WMD before resorting to force.

I have taken part in only one top secret mission but it

features in a book by Bob Woodward, so I feel comfortable writing about it. In August 2002, Jack felt that the US, dragging the UK behind it, was fixed on a belligerent course. The case for action was clear enough to the president and his inner circle; they were not much interested in the views of others. Jack did not think the international community, and in particular the United Nations, should be sidestepped. At short notice, he requested a meeting with Colin Powell, secretary of state.

Powell was on holiday with his wife, Alma, at the Long Island home of Ronald Lauder and his wife, Jo. At the northern tip of Long Island, the mega-rich have gorgeous holiday homes which they quaintly call cottages. The Lauder place was among the most isolated, because Lauder had methodically acquired all parts of the view from his cottage, buying swathes of shoreline and potato field as they came up for sale. It was a peaceful retreat for the Powells, but they agreed to disturb their rest to see Jack, who took with him one detective and me.

We had lunch with the Lauders and then settled down to do business over coffee. Powell agreed that I should take the record for both sides, so only three of us sat down on the veranda. They concluded that, grave though the threat from Saddam Hussein might be, to move against him without the explicit backing of the United Nations would be a mistake. Legitimacy was vital to international acceptance of military action, and only the Security Council could confer legitimacy. Powell would report to the president that a Security Council Resolution was of paramount importance to the UK.

Over the following weeks, the US side accepted that the UN would be central to their plans, which the president spelled out explicitly when he addressed the General Assembly in New York on 12 September. As sometimes seems to happen when exact wording is vital and changes are being brokered until the speaker stands up to deliver a speech, Bush's printed text omitted key words but, having been personally involved in the textual negotiation, he was able to extemporise and add them as he spoke. Later he told Jack that, as he surveyed the sea of faces in the packed and cavernous hall, he spotted Jack, sitting directly behind the United Kingdom name plate. When the audience was so large, it helped him to focus on one person and, in effect, deliver a speech to that one person; Bush said he had given his UN speech to Jack.

The work initiated at the General Assembly led to SCR 1441, adopted unanimously by the Security Council on 8 November 2002. The main sticking point, which Bush's speech had acknowledged, was how many resolutions were needed before military action. But, as Jeremy Greenstock said at the time, if the US and UK had been content to concede multiple resolutions then the negotiation would have been a whole lot quicker. It was precisely because they needed text that allowed the possibility of military action without further recourse to the Council that the negotiation took six weeks rather than six hours.

Until the invasion started in March 2003, Jack looked for diplomatic means to end the crisis. He attended three ministerial meetings in New York, at the first of which Colin Powell attempted to emulate Adlai Stevenson's tour de force at the height of the Cuban Missile Crisis, by presenting irrefutable evidence to the Security Council of Iraqi wrongdoing. In the days before his hour-long briefing, Powell spoke by phone to Jack (I listened in; private secretaries are often silently in the background, taking the record). Powell sounded confident of the strength of the intelligence on which he would rest his case, slam-dunk evidence of Iraqi possession of, and intent to use, WMD. By the time he made his presentation, he would have examined it all with a fine-toothed comb; he hoped to sway the waverers on the Council.

When Powell spoke on 5 February, I was sitting behind Jack Straw, looking across at Powell. Usually, the American and British delegations sit side by side (only the occasional Council membership of the United Republic of Tanzania can separate them). The president of the Council always sits in the middle of the horseshoe-shaped table, with the secretary-general to her or his left. At the end of a month-long presidency, everyone (apart from the secretary-general) shifts one place anti-clockwise. With Germany in the chair, the UK and US occupied the places at the ends of the horseshoe's prongs in February 2003. Powell looked Jack in the eye as he delivered his remarks. As he made his case, I noted it was thinner than promised; the slam-dunk evidence was missing. It did not persuade Dominique de Villepin (French foreign minister) or any other waverer.

The fact is that positions on all sides were entrenched and unyielding long before the House of Commons debate on 17 March. Most countries, including close allies, wanted a second resolution; France and Russia had made plain their unwillingness to grant a second resolution any time soon. That being the case, the Commons debated authorising military action on the basis only of SCR 1441.

The most memorable speech was Robin Cook's, delivered from the back benches, explaining why he had resigned from the government earlier that day. It was meticulously argued and passionately delivered but, as Jack explained to me in his Commons office after the House had divided 412 to 149 in favour of the government's motion, its brilliance was irrelevant: even before the debate, the Opposition and the overwhelming majority of the parliamentary Labour Party were convinced that the PM had done all he could reasonably be expected to do in order to avoid conflict.

Hostilities started on 23 March. Saddam Hussein fell from power on 9 April, his monumental bronze statue toppled in Paradise Square the same day. Almost as quick as the military victory was the discovery that the casus belli did not exist. Robin Cook had been right: Saddam Hussein's regime had no viable WMD.

Going to war in March 2003 on a false prospectus was the worst intelligence failure in my career. MI6 is still recovering from the wounds inflicted by Richard Dearlove's working methods. As head of MI6, Richard had direct access to the prime minister, able to slip unobserved into Number 10 by the back door. In their meetings in the winter of 2002–3, he assured Blair of the accuracy of the intelligence on which Blair was basing his decisions; subsequent events proved that Richard's confidence was misplaced.

We know now that Iraqi officials habitually lied to each other about the size and capabilities of their WMD. They may or may not have guessed that Western intelligence agencies were eavesdropping, but without doubt they feared that other parts of their own system were listening to their phone calls and they knew what they had to say to each other even in private.

Once committed to a particular course, it proved easier to follow through rather than correct it. After the initial military victory, the coalition took over the country, overtly accepting that it was the occupying power. Iraqis, including those otherwise sympathetic to the coalition's aims, were horrified. Outsiders having decapitated an unloved regime, they would (as their ambassador to the UK later told me) have preferred to be left alone to sort themselves out 'in the traditional way'. They knew the power centres that had to be satisfied better than any outsider; they knew their politics was more complicated than Ahmed Chalabi persuasively presented to Vice President Cheney.

Instead, the US, backed by the UK, doubled down. The coalition embraced the responsibility of an occupying power, stated baldly in Security Council resolutions. Iraqis were denied the fig leaf they needed to disguise their powerlessness and be able to lead the task of reconstruction.

Instead Paul Bremer was installed, effectively as an American viceroy, at the head of the Coalition Provisional Authority (CPA). CPA Orders 1 and 2 abolished the Ba'ath Party and dismantled Iraq's military, security, and intelligence infrastructure and effectively sowed the seeds of the coalition's ultimate failure. The CPA decided to start from scratch. Powell popularised the Pottery Barn rule – 'You break it, you own it' – but the Administration learned the hard way that all the time and money in the world was not enough for outsiders to reassemble a smashed Iraq.

In politics, decisions are often taken much earlier in a process than people outside that process realise. Blair committed the UK irrevocably to support the US in any conflict before Jack or the rest of the cabinet realised. Not everything was written down; in no era has everything important been written down. Quiet understandings, without witnesses, resting solely on the trust between the parties involved, have always been important. I note that, from early on in the long run-up to the Iraq War, President Bush talked and behaved as if the UK was his most dependable ally. In this case, there is a key piece of written evidence: John Chilcot unearthed a personal letter from Blair to Bush written in July 2002, in which the prime minister assured the president, 'I will be with you, whatever.' Subsequent events justified the confidence Bush evidently placed in that private promise.

Iraq and Afghanistan took up most of the Blair government's foreign policy attention, but the most consequential foreign policy decisions for the future of the UK were on Europe policy.

After the end of the Cold War, the UK decided to support the integration of former Warsaw Pact countries into the West as quickly as possible. Although some in the US hesitated, the UK advocated NATO membership for Poland, Czechoslovakia (later Czech Republic and Slovakia), Hungary, Romania, Bulgaria, and the Baltic states from the start. The GDR had become a member on the day of German unification, 3 October 1990.

UK policymakers crafted the criteria for membership for an organisation whose purpose had been to defend its members against the alliance of which these countries had recently been a part.

There were three: that joining should be the desire of the overwhelming majority of their citizens; that they should be able to contribute to the collective defence of the alliance; and that their membership should enhance the overall security of Europe (code for: would not be taken as a hostile act by Moscow). Western leaders never acted as if Russia were fundamentally different from the Soviet Union – Russia was the last plausible adversary in Europe. For the rest, NATO invented Membership Action Plans (MAPs) to guide the process and mark the progress of applicant states.

By 2004, all the original list of aspirant members, plus Slovenia, had joined. But Russia was finding its feet again. Putin reassessed Russia's situation, and he decided to do something about it. One of the rewards for Russia's acceptance of the dissolution of the Soviet Union was inclusion in the G7. The economic case for the G8 was thin; Russian inclusion was all about the politics. But as Putin changed his mind about the usefulness to Russia of rapprochement with the West, so its presence in the G8 became obviously more anomalous. They did not agree with anyone else about anything important.

Tony Blair's final G8 Summit was at Heiligendamm in June 2007. I was invited as part of my preparations for becoming Gordon Brown's foreign policy adviser. Blair's most interesting meeting was with Putin. Knowing that this was their final meeting as heads of government, Putin decided to set the record straight, or rather to set out his reinterpretation of history: since the end of the Cold War the West had taken Russia for a ride, it had exploited Russia's moment of weakness. That moment was coming to an end. In the future, Russia would be more assertive, defending and promoting its interests. He developed the themes he had launched at the Munich Security Conference earlier in the year: Russia was back and everyone else had better show it more respect.

Putin has been as good as his word. Since then, the conflicts festering in most of the republics of the former Soviet Union have got worse, starting with Georgia in 2008. Russia grabbed Crimea in 2014 and attempted to snuff out Ukraine in 2022. It has also been more active externally, coming to the rescue of its Ba'athist allies in Syria in 2015. Russia has also ensured that the Security Council barely functions, when it is at odds (that is to say, most of the time) with what the US, France, and the UK want to achieve.

In response, the West more or less maintained its course. NATO kept its door open: Albania and Croatia joined in 2009, Montenegro in 2017 and North Macedonia in 2020 (shortly after the thorny issue of its name was resolved). But Merkel made allies think again at NATO's Bucharest Summit in 2008. Spurred on by President Bush, leaders were on the point of extending MAPs to Ukraine and Georgia, as far as Washington was concerned, their membership was the logical conclusion of the West's victory. Merkel reminded colleagues of the conditions of membership; it was not at all clear that NATO membership was the settled choice of the majority of the population. It was even less clear that Ukrainian and Georgian armed forces were capable of contributing significantly to their own defence or that their membership would enhance Europe's overall security. Enlargement to include countries that Russia had traditionally viewed as Russian spheres of influence needed more careful consideration.

Merkel prevailed. MAPs were withheld. The aspirant governments did not get the concrete proof of a path to membership that they wanted. But the principle that they could (indeed were one day expected to) become members was enshrined in the Summit communiqué.

The Bucharest Summit was a seminal moment, the point when some allies, led by Germany, began to see that victory in the Cold War had been bigger than the West needed it to be, and that the West had exploited that victory without fully thinking through its consequences. The West did not need the Soviet Union to disintegrate in order to confirm or consolidate the victory. Indeed, disintegration gave Moscow a grievance that Russians everywhere might feel was an affront, even a new fact that had to be reversed.

Promises made in the flush of victory have to be honoured. The three Baltic states are all full members of NATO; their defence is covered by Article 5; their border with Russia is the brightest red line. But there is a difference between the Baltics states and other components of the former Soviet Union: none of the others is an ally; none is covered by Article 5. Our obligations are fewer. We will help Ukraine and Georgia: we might sanction Russia; we might supply materiel and military training to Kyiv. But we will not fight alongside Ukrainians and Georgians. Politicians and policymakers in the West should not mislead their own public, nor the people of Ukraine and Georgia, by implying or promising more.

The process to join the European Union was more exacting, and existing member state hesitation more difficult to overcome. But on 1 May 2004, the EU admitted eight Eastern European countries (Czech Republic, Estonia, Hungary, Latvia, Lithuania, Poland, Slovakia, and Slovenia) plus two Mediterranean island states (Cyprus and Malta) in its biggest ever enlargement. Bulgaria and Romania followed on 1 January 2007 and Croatia on 1 July 2013.

As prime minister, Gordon Brown once asked his foreign affairs private secretary what the FCO had achieved strategically over the previous decade. At the time, he did not take issue with the answer: to get the former countries of the Warsaw Pact into the EU and NATO before Russia could object effectively. But official British enthusiasm for enlargement clouded the judgement of British negotiators. Other member states, more aware that political rather than economic facts were driving the process, insisted on long transition times before key parts of the *acquis* came into force, particularly freedom of movement.

In the UK, officials reckoned that perhaps 14,000 Poles would move to the UK in the first year when freedom of movement was allowed. The political wish to signal a warm welcome and equality within democratic Europe was strong enough for Home Office objections to be overruled. Unique among existing member states, the UK allowed full freedom of movement from the day Poland and the rest became members states.

The exact number of Poles who eventually came to the UK is disputed but was at least fifty times the initial forecast. Over the following decade almost 5% of the population of Lithuania relocated to the UK. By the time of the renegotiation in 2016, up to 40% of newly qualified Bulgarian doctors were working in the UK.

Migration was the most widely discussed issue during the UK's referendum campaign about EU membership. But British problems with the EU went much deeper. The UK was not present at the creation. The British stood back when the European Coal and Steel Community was formed in 1951, and held back again when the Six met at the Messina Conference in 1955. But an under-secretary at the Board of Trade attended several meetings of the Spaak Committee, launched after Messina, which prepared the ground for the Treaty of Rome in 1957 and formation of the EEC in 1958. Leaving his final meeting, the under-secretary Russell Bretherton is alleged to have quipped (revealing more perhaps about the Frenchman who attributed the quotation to him): 'Gentlemen, you are trying to negotiate something which you will never be able to negotiate. But, if negotiated, it will not be ratified. And, if ratified, it will not work. Au revoir and bonne chance.'

Throughout the 1950s, the British economy remained the second biggest in the world. Memory of victory in the Second World War was even stronger than it is today. The UK still had an empire. Although India and Pakistan gained independence in 1947, and Ceylon (Sri Lanka) in 1948, Ghana was the only other colony to gain independence by the time the Treaty of Rome was signed by Belgium, France,

West Germany, Italy, Luxembourg, and the Netherlands.

Britons did not feel they needed Europe, nor that they belonged in Europe. Churchill, a passionate advocate of European union for Europeans who were not British, toyed with the lofty idea of the Anglo-sphere, of strengthening the bonds between English-speaking nations. But forces unleashed by the First World War (the American advocacy of self-determination and intolerance of colonialism) and the Second World War (the impoverishment and international decline of the UK) could not be ignored. In the end, governments could not resist them.

When Harold Macmillan became prime minister in 1957 in the aftermath of the Suez disaster, he ordered a review of the UK's international options. It concluded that a closer economic and political relationship with Europe (our neighbourhood) offered the best hope for our economic recovery and continued political influence. Macmillan accepted the conclusion and, on 1 August 1961, applied for membership of the EEC.

The first two applications ended with French vetoes (Harold Wilson applied a second time in 1967). The French and other existing member states felt that it was for the applicant rather than the institution the applicant aspired to join to adapt itself.

Failing to be present at the creation had consequences for the UK throughout all application processes and throughout UK membership. One reason why joining became more urgent was the fact that, while we were outside, in the words of a middle-ranking official of the time, 'the EEC behaved like a complete bastard towards us'. Undaunted by de Gaulle (and spurred by his resignation in January 1969) the UK explored the option of a third application in 1969. When Edward Heath became prime minister the next year, bringing that negotiation to a successful conclusion was his government's top priority.

Heath was among the last British politicians to have personal experience of fighting in the Second World War. He was absolutely determined to make the UK part of an organisation whose main purpose was to make another war in Europe impossible. In his long retirement, Helmut Schmidt used to ask young visitors what the point of the EU was and would patiently correct verbose answers with the single word 'peace'.

Such was Heath's determination to support the EU's founding objective that he sanctioned compromises in all parts of the negotiation that his predecessors balked at. In particular, he accepted the EEC's funding model and agriculture policy, which (unlike in the UK) guaranteed farmers a certain price for their produce. Georges Pompidou (de Gaulle's successor) got what he wanted, but his success meant that the new member state was never fully reconciled to the demands of membership: in the 1970s, the UK vociferously objected to the 'wine lakes' and 'butter mountains'; in the 1980s, Mrs Thatcher noisily shifted the focus to, 'We want our money back!' Unhappy with parts of the existing project which it had been forced to accept, the UK energetically resisted most plans to expand EEC/EU areas of competence. The most prominent exception was the single market, conceived and driven to fruition by a commissioner, Arthur Cockfield, nominated by Margaret Thatcher.

Having held back from joining the euro at its launch (the most significant of the new plans), UK membership looked increasingly semi-detached. The UK did not like Eurozone countries caucusing before EU meetings but, in relevant policy areas, could not object effectively. Historians will, I suspect, look back and see that the writing was on the wall long before the migration crisis that followed the accession of the A10 in 2004 and was exacerbated by refugee flows from Syria, Iraq, and Afghanistan in the summer of 2015.

As long as the UK was a member, some of the design flaws of the EU were held in check, or at least did not make themselves felt. The UK never wavered on the primacy of member states over EU institutions and on the primacy of the practical over the theoretical. Before the issue of UK membership went critical, the state secretary at the Auswärtiges Amt (the German Federal Foreign Office) told me that the UK performed an essential function for the EU: 'You are a reliable bullshit-o-meter, consistently and unerringly calling out what will not work, what's unnecessary, and what's extravagant.'

Now the UK is not in the EU, I wonder how the fundamental flaws will develop, three in particular:

- The democratic deficit;
- The uncertainty over *finalité* (the final political and economic arrangements between EU institutions and member states); and
- The unresolved tension between France and Germany, now overwhelmingly the two biggest and most important member states.

In a different context, Tip O'Neill, former speaker of the House of Representatives, observed that 'all politics is local'. However debatable his insight, I would add that 'almost no politics is transnational'. Citizens need to feel connected to their leaders. Part of that is that they literally need to speak the same language. If your ministers speak a different language from you, the people they are trying to govern, you cannot immediately understand them; they will always feel remote and less legitimate.

From the start, the EEC/EU has been aware of its democratic deficit. The Treaty of Rome makes provision for a European Parliament (EP) in an effort to connect ordinary citizens to those at the European level taking decisions that affect them. For two decades the EP was comprised of delegates from the national parliaments of member states. To the theorists, this did not involve ordinary citizens enough so, in 1979, and every five years since then, the EP has held direct elections.

The resulting parliament now has 705 members, drawn from 140 different political parties, speaking twenty-three different official languages. Knowledge of proceedings in the EP is almost non-existent in most member states. Knowing little of what happens there or how it affects their lives, voters are far less engaged than when voting in national elections. Mostly, they do not vote. Voter participation is highest in Germany (48% in 2019) and lowest in Slovakia (13%).

None of the EU's leaders is directly elected: the presidents of the Commission, the European Council, the European Parliament, and the European Central Bank are generally chosen by heads of state and government meeting at the European Council. Political considerations rather than the personal qualities and qualifications of candidates for high office are key: a balance between north and south, east and west, new and old member states, men and women, with pre-eminence of centre-right (EPP) or centre-left (S&D) in the European Council overriding all other factors. Over the decades, Luxembourgers have done disproportionately well; newer member states (that is to say, those that joined after 1995) are still doing embarrassingly badly. With such thin legitimacy, you might expect appointees to behave with a certain modesty or restraint; actual behaviour more resembles a prime minister returned to power in a landslide.

Europe, stubbornly, is still not one demos. Although an increasing number of Europeans are comfortable with more than one identity, the European identity is still weak for the overwhelming majority of EU citizens. The countries where the EU identity is strongest are either small (Luxembourg) or have weak national institutions (Belgium). The enthusiasm of eurocrats from these nations for the European project has so far failed to convince or energise the rest.

That is an unpromising backdrop to a push for further integration but, if history is a guide, that will not prevent the integrationists from trying. They argue that more integration will make the rationale of the project clearer and more easily explicable to more people.

Which brings me to the challenge of *finalité*. Again, this has been present and recognised since the start. Signatories to the Treaty of Rome were at the start of a journey whose destination they deliberately left unclear. Over sixty years later, the question of ultimate destination is still unanswered. Whenever it is mentioned, the most ambitious options are routinely ruled out. At the moment, few prominent politicians publicly advocate a United States of Europe, with member states analogous to states in the US.

And yet the EU continues to grow in a way that is compatible with an eventual United States of Europe. One striking example is the European External Action Service. The EU is the only international institution that insists, in order to have any relationship with a third country at all, that its diplomatic representatives are treated like diplomats from a sovereign state.

In order to cause trouble, British newspapers will from time to time run stories about France giving up its permanent seat on the UN Security Council, to be replaced by an EU seat. It is customarily French diplomats who most energetically deny the possibility, pointing out (for the rest of the world, as well as the rest of the EU) that such an arrangement would diminish the EU's presence on the Security Council. Usually, three EU member states are members of the Security Council (in 2021, Estonia, France, and Ireland); 6% of the world's population has 20% of Security Council seats.

The idea of a European Army has also resurfaced. The French rejected the notion in the 1950s, but President Macron pushes the idea of 'strategic autonomy'. Trump showed that the US could not always be relied upon. I see two problems from Europe's point of view. First, defence is a serious business. Right now, the US supplies at least 40% of NATO's capabilities. If the US withdrew from

NATO, these key capabilities would have to be expensively replaced. No European country seems willing (or, indeed, able) to fill that gap.

Second, the rationale for a continued large US presence in Europe, nearly eighty years after the end of the Second World War and over thirty years after the end of the Cold War, gets weaker from the US point of view (which was why Trump found a ready domestic audience for his views). Americans stay because they are made to feel welcome; Europeans have always vociferously assured them that their presence is vital to wider international security. When that ceases to be the case, US enthusiasm for staying will wane rapidly. In 2022, Russia's invasion of Ukraine rekindled western European enthusiasm for NATO. Under pressure from Chancellor Scholz, Macron has diluted his ambition to the less-hostile-to-America 'European strategic sovereignty'. But danger still lurks: the US may yet take the French at their word and disappear (a) before they are invited to leave and (b) before Europe is ready to take up the slack.

Third, and most important, the first duty of a state is to provide security for its citizens. The most difficult decision any government has to take is whether to deploy its young people in order to defend the national interest, when everyone understands that some of those young people may die in the action. Parliamentary debates to endorse military deployments are the best attended, most serious, and most consequential. Members of Parliament rarely agree unanimously but all of them explicitly recognise that, despite personal misgivings or opposition, they are bound by the result. And their country feels the same way – voters trusting their legislators with the lives of their young people is one of the defining features of a legitimate parliament.

To date, only parliaments of nation states can claim that legitimacy. Max Weber defined the state as the unit of government that has a monopoly on the use of legitimate force. In no country do voters show any openness to the idea that the supranational level should assume that responsibility. Logically, a European Army would be deployed with the agreement of the European Parliament rather than the parliaments of member states. But I cannot imagine the youth of, say, Hungary, being deployed in opposition to the wishes of the Hungarian Parliament. No doubt decisions on deployment might be subject to the agreement of national parliaments, but in that case the army would not be truly European. On security matters, the national level remains stubbornly vibrant.

Over time, the shortcomings of Eurozone governance are making themselves apparent. The fiscally responsible have always been impatient with the ill-disciplined: 'Grexit' was a word before 'Brexit'. During the climax of the Greek financial crisis in 2011, I found senior German officials unsympathetic to the Greek government. Lucas Papademos, who led a government of national unity formed to deal with the early stages of the crisis, had previously been governor of the Bank of Greece (1994–2002). Some Germans blamed him for cooking the books to make it appear that the drachma was qualified to join the euro at its inception, when subsequent events proved that it manifestly was not.

For different reasons, the French and Germans are unhappy in private with the functioning of the euro. The French hanker after a Eurozone budget with a Eurozone finance minister presiding over it. The Germans think that euro governance is weighted too much in favour of the small and more frequently wayward. Their arguments and hesitations cancel each other out. The euro is far more resilient than its critics at the outset predicted, but its long-term success still does not appear guaranteed.

The central bargain at the heart of the EEC/EU is between France and Germany. Both countries were left shattered by the Second World War: 25 June 1940 is the most infamous date in French history, when France capitulated without a proper fight, and the Third Reich is the most infamous prolonged episode in German history, an aberration for whose sins Germany will always atone. In the 1950s, France wanted to rebuild and Germany wanted to be readmitted to the human race. The ECSC and EEC were the means they chose.

Strategically, the EEC/EU sits on a continuum of French international ambition. Since Cardinal Richelieu, France – having ended the religious wars which were the bloodiest conflict in its history – has sought to dominate the continent of Europe. Louis XIV was successful and Napoleon was spectacularly successful for a time in realising this ambition.

Over the centuries, creeping German unification was the most potent obstacle to French ambition. At the Peace of Westphalia in 1648, more than 300 entities calling themselves German exercised some degree of sovereignty.

Napoleon, when he abolished the Holy Roman Empire and mediatised most sovereign princes, swept away many of the smaller entities. The Congress of Vienna cut down the number still further. By the time the German Empire was declared in the Hall of Mirrors at the Palace of Versailles in 1871, there were four kingdoms, six grand duchies, five duchies, seven principalities, and three free and Hanseatic cities. Although these twenty-five constituent parts never surrendered all powers to the imperial level, the imperial level was decisive in foreign and defence policy. Over the next half century, a united Germany proved too big for the rest of Europe's comfort.

Even when Germany was at its lowest ebb, with total defeat at the end of total war, the *Wirtschaftswunder* was just around the corner. As early as the 1950s, it was clear that the Federal Republic would one day have the biggest and strongest economy in Europe.

The French sought to harness that power on French terms. Throughout the first half of my career, commentators' favourite simile was a tandem bicycle: France steering at the front with Germany pedalling furiously behind.

From the days of Schuman and Adenauer, both France and Germany have talked passionately about the need for and benefits of reconciliation. They have signed treaties to underline their intent, most notably the Élysée Treaty on 22 January 1963.

In 2013, I was in Berlin when France and Germany celebrated the fiftieth anniversary of the Élysée Treaty in style. All members of the Assemblée nationale were invited to the Reichstag, which was refitted for the occasion. Normally,

Norman Foster's refurbished building has seating enough only for members of the Bundestag (a varying number but so far never more than 736). Every five years, all those purple seats are unscrewed from their moorings and replaced by smaller black seats to allow all members of the Federal Convention (whose sole task is to elect the Federal President) a place to sit.

On 22 January 2013, in the huge hemicycle configured for a Federal Convention, over a thousand delegates, 50% French and 50% German, took their seats. They gathered to celebrate a treaty whose main provisions concerned cultural and educational exchange. What struck me, sitting in the gallery with other diplomats, was that every speaker (with a few exceptions, including Wolfgang Schäuble, born and brought up in Freiburg, close to the French border) spoke their own language, and that, for every speech, half the audience wore earphones in order to hear a translation.

The next day, a Bundestag member complained to me that dinner afterwards had been no better – his table had required the services of interpreters throughout: 'Most French politicians don't even speak English.'

Fifty years had failed to affect the cultural or educational priorities of either side. English is Germany's second language, and vies with Spanish to be France's. Although both countries may worry most about each other, their actions show that in the end they care more about other international relationships, particularly with the United States.

Each French attempt to channel German power to the benefit of French objectives has failed to constrain Germany. The most recent example is the euro. In private, François

Mitterrand was as sceptical of the benefits of German unification as Margaret Thatcher was in public. Before publicly embracing unification, he extracted German agreement to launching a single EU currency. The idea of a single currency had been part of the founding fathers' vision, most recently pushed by Jacques Delors when he was president of the Commission. Despite Germans' attachment to the Deutschmark, Chancellor Kohl accepted Mitterrand's condition (and claimed naming rights).

But, once again, France failed to clip Germany's wings. Even fixing the governance of the new currency and consistently denying Germany the presidency of the ECB failed to prevent Germany from becoming the euro's principal beneficiary. A single currency has reduced German transaction costs with its main supply chain, that is to say, the rest of the Eurozone.

With a new chancellor in Germany, President Macron spies a new opening for French leadership in Europe. That he was the best candidate to exploit that opportunity was a key promise in his re-election campaign.

For a time, Blair aspired to that role. Although he outlasted President Chirac by only one month (and Chirac had preceded him in high office by two years), Blair was plausibly the leader of the pack in Europe after his second election victory in 2001. He wanted to be the first full-time president of the European Council. To show himself willing, he was more accommodating than his chancellor wanted him to be in the negotiation that preceded the signing of the multi-annual framework (for 2007–13) on 17 May 2006. The Commission and other member states targeted the UK rebate and Blair yielded, trading in part of the rebate in order to ease overall agreement. Personal ambition appears to have trumped national interest.

In the end, the concession did not help. By the time the decision was taken, the centre-right rather than centre-left was dominant on the European Council and Gordon Brown was not exactly the most impassioned advocate of the idea. Herman Van Rompuy (prime minister of Belgium) got the job, and Catherine Ashton became the first high representative for foreign affairs and security policy by way of compensation for the UK.

Working at the centre, I learned as much about how government works as about the policy issues government was tackling. The buildings, geography, and history of power all influence how cabinet ministers work. Number 10 has as profound an effect on British politicians and civil servants as St Peter's does on Roman Catholics. I crossed its threshold for the first time in 2000, delivering a letter from Jack to the prime minister. I was surprised to discover that the number is painted on the shiny black of the panelled door. Later, I found out that the door is metal rather than wood, and is an exact replica of the original door, which was upgraded after the IRA attacked Downing Street in 1991. The original is displayed in the Churchill War Rooms.

The building is an elegant town house, built by George Downing on land granted to him by Charles II in 1682. In common with many speculative ventures, it was more important for it to look good than to be solid. Maintenance has been a challenge from the start, made worse by modern security requirements. After IRA mortars damaged the white drawing room and cabinet room in 1991, all windows were replaced with custom-made replicas in sturdier materials with blast-proof glass, which was so much heavier than the originals that an existing subsidence problem measurably accelerated.

Despite its shortcomings, its occupants love the place. Although it is surprisingly big for a London terraced house (the front building is connected to a larger house behind, overlooking Horse Guards Parade), the formal rooms are few. The pillared cabinet room is austere, dominated by a coffin-shaped table (designed by Harold Macmillan, so he could see all his cabinet colleagues) with only one portrait (Walpole), one English landscape, and a sideboard with a Saudi sword, which King Fahd presented to John Major on the signing of the Al Yamamah defence contract.

Next to the cabinet room, through a huge pair of blue panelled doors, is the office that most prime ministers have used as their own, the 'den'. And beyond that is a larger office, where traditionally the four most senior civil servants plus one duty clerk sat. When Patrick worked in Number 10, fewer than 100 people worked in the building. These days, the overall numbers have ballooned to more than 400. Proximity to the prime minister is prized. The chief of staff (a political appointee, the first being Jonathan Powell) has displaced the principal private secretary from the desk closest to the den. Subject area private secretaries have proliferated and been distributed around the building, but all are less than a thirty-second walk to the den.

Apart from the cabinet room, the state rooms are on the first floor. The white drawing room sits in the corner.

It has the best pictures, including two paintings by J. M. W. Turner, which have been there since the 1980s. Visiting Paris, Mrs Thatcher was intrigued to see these paintings adorning the walls of the British Residence; she wondered why the ambassador to Paris should have better pictures than the head of government and 'requested' their relocation to Downing Street.

Repairing and restoring the building is a never-ending task. Most occupants do not stay long enough to have a significant impact, beyond leaving their portrait on the wall of the main staircase when they leave. When Mrs Thatcher arrived, she was shocked at how dowdy it was. A carpet was designed for the corridors and communal spaces (so expensive that it had to be ordered in stages, the last section being fitted under Theresa May). She commissioned Quinlan Terry to install an ornate ceiling in the white drawing room (in the restoration that followed the IRA attack, one small patch was left unrepaired to serve as a reminder). And she had the larger room next to the white drawing room painted terracotta, giving it its modern name, and acquiesced in the inclusion of a thatcher in the stucco above the doorframe into the pillared room.

Although Mrs Thatcher remains the prime minister to exert greatest influence over the look of the building, the prime minister whose spirit hangs heaviest over the place is Winston Churchill. His favourite armchair still sits in the inner hall, and a bronze statue of him and Clementine has no fixed position but is always somewhere in the building. He is the only prime minister to have two portraits on the main staircase: one between Neville Chamberlain and Clement Attlee, and the black-and-white Yousuf Karsh photograph, taken in the Speaker's Chamber in Ottawa, with Churchill glowering at the photographer who had just taken away the cigar he had been smoking. The Karsh never moves from its place on the landing near the den.

While working for Gordon Brown, I got to know Martin Gilbert. Martin told me that, after Randolph Churchill had asked him to help write his father's biography in 1962, he had got to know every prime minister well. At one point in the 1960s, a Conservative PM and a Labour PM had both offered him a safe seat to represent their party. They had all been interested in the minutiae of Churchill's life, how he had arranged his day, how he had worked, and how he had paced himself.

Churchill was the last British prime minister to affect the course of world history. He saw – more articulately than anyone else – the threats posed by Nazism and Soviet Communism. He had inspired people with his words. Although spectacularly flawed, overall his personal impact was positive. Number 10 and the House of Commons were the backdrop to the main events in his public life. All Churchill's successors have lived in his shadow, conscious that they are working in the same places he did, conscious of what they have in common, and hoping to emulate him – to be forgiven their failings because they achieve something undeniably historic.

Even though he was prime minister in the UK's darkest hour, Churchill was fortunate in the 1940s in having a single objective on which everyone around him and everyone in the country agreed: 'Victory at all costs, victory in spite of all terror, victory however long and hard the road may be; for without victory, there is no survival.' In the 1950s, his second administration was as beset by squabbling and factions pursuing multiple, incompatible agendas as any other.

Fighting for the PM's ear often seems like the main pre-occupation of other workers in Downing Street. The way to look at Number 10 that will best help your understanding of what life is like there is to think of it as a royal court. The prime minister is the sovereign and all power flows from them. Everybody serves at the PM's pleasure, even when the PM is weak or wrong. Over time, everybody around the PM seems to relate to them like a courtier to a monarch. King Henry VIII and the later Louis are helpful guides.

There is generally a consort and a mistress – well, someone of the opposite sex who fulfils the policy role of Anne Boleyn or Madame de Pompadour, if not the bedroom role. Consorts can choose to be passive or active in government. Denis Thatcher, Norma Major, Samantha Cameron, and Philip May were all passive in politics: hugely important support for the PM but able to help by being unequivocally in their spouse's corner without trying to interfere directly in the boxing bout. With no great controversy, all but Mrs Cameron received a knighthood or damehood from their spouse's successor as PM.

Cherie Booth, Sarah Brown, and Carrie Johnson were all more active. Like the foreign-born spouse of a Bourbon king, such active consorts cannot assume that the rest of the court will accept their activism. They are most effective when they target their interventions and take up causes ordinarily associated with junior members of the royal family (social, environmental), building alliances with cabinet ministers rather than challenging them. Like their eighteenth-century predecessors, they are most influential when it comes to appointments.

I have no idea and no interest in whether the 'mistress' figures have sex with their prime minister. But like Madame de Maintenon at Versailles, they exert huge influence and are stalwart props, especially in times of crisis. They are out-of-hours figures; they know the boss's moods and how and when to make a case. They attract a lot of envy but also respect, because they can get things done when others cannot. Harold Wilson had Marcia Falkender; Margaret Thatcher, Charles Powell; John Major, Sarah Hogg; Tony Blair, Anji Hunter; Gordon Brown, Sue Nye; David Cameron, Liz Sugg; Theresa May had Gavin Barwell and Boris Johnson – well, he married his mistress.

Next in proximity are the body servants. King Henry VIII had a Groom of the Stool, and Gordon Brown had Helen Etheridge and Leeanne Johnston to ensure he always had a clean shirt and make-up ready for his close-up. Unflinchingly performing relatively menial tasks is part of the body servants' lot. Mrs Landingham in the NBC TV series *The West Wing* was the über-body servant. The body servants tend to have greater longevity than the rotating cast of royal favourites.

Royal favourites, never elected, never bequeathed from one administration to the next, generally don't last long. The most spectacular recent example was Dominic

Cummings. Generally, the relationship ends with a rift and hurt feelings, but the Johnson/Cummings split set a new standard for noise and acrimony.

The favourite's job is to stir things up. Even though prime ministers sit atop a system programmed to respond to them, they do not feel that; they feel resistance or reluctance. They feel the need to prove that someone new is in charge, someone who will not be bamboozled or slow rolled. They send forth the favourite to disrupt, and to get the system to attune itself to their priorities and way of doing things.

Theresa May had Nick Timothy and Fiona McLeod Hill, Cameron had Steve Hilton (for a time), Brown had Shriti Vadera, Blair had Alastair Campbell. Favourites all know the system somewhat, generally because they have been with their boss in a ministry before Number 10, but experience shows that none of them knows the system well enough to get it to act quickly. They behave like Mr Kirrane's wind in the fable, and they generally blow themselves out. The fact that all prime ministers feel they need such a figure is instructive; clearly, the status quo feels sclerotic and unresponsive. The Civil Service could be better at building bridges with these figures.

At some point, prime ministers are always hit by squalls or languish in the doldrums. Whenever this happens, the call goes up, in the House or the editorials of a supportive newspaper, for them to change their team in Number 10. Even if it is nothing else, change is a distraction from substantive problems, so sometimes the team is changed. The favourites, because of their public profile and conspicuous activity, are usually first in line to receive their P45. But sacking staff when the boss is the problem never works.

Prime ministers need a Number 10 team that works for them. The key appointments are personal – they need to be made by the PM with the help of advisers he or she trusts. And then these appointees need to get on with the job, as an extension of the PM. When they are doing the job well, they are indistinguishable from the PM, an extension of the PM, to the point where there is no greater point in taking issue with them than taking issue with the PM's kneecaps or elbows. Taking issue with the advisers is really taking issue with the PM, because – when they are good – they speak authoritatively for their boss rather than themselves.

Just as there is overlap between mistress and royal favourite (who do not have to be the opposite gender from the PM), so there is overlap between royal favourite and wise counsellor from before the premiership. The wise counsellors are those who give a PM the most help in assembling the rest of their core team. Johnson had Ed Lister, Cameron had Kate Fall and Ed Llewellyn, Brown had Ed Balls, and Blair had Derry Irvine and Charlie Falconer. Sometimes these advisers go into the Commons and the cabinet; usually they end up in the Lords.

Last are the hired hands, there to do a particular job. I was one of Gordon Brown's hired hands, there to give foreign policy advice. More particularly, as I learned from the *Evening Standard* early in my tenure, I was there to 'Get us out of Iraq, in as good order as possible (but to get us out, no matter what) without pissing off the Americans too much.' I was the least prominent of the Three Amigos, the others being Jeremy Heywood* (responsible for domestic policy) and Jon Cunliffe (responsible for economic and international financial policy).

The hired hands are a subset of the most numerous group, the permanent civil servants, who quietly pass from one administration to the next, serving the prime minister of the day, whoever she or he is. The grandest of the permanent establishment is the cabinet secretary. For the century after Maurice Hankey invented the job for himself in the middle of the First World War, prime ministers accepted whoever was sitting in the fine wood-panelled office in William Kent's Cabinet Office building: by definition, its occupant was able and had been tested. All parties were familiar with and comfortable with the idea of 'serial loyalty': just because Robert Armstrong had been Harold Wilson's PPS did not mean he could not, with complete discretion and faithfulness, be cabinet secretary for Margaret Thatcher. Nowadays, anyone aspiring to be cabinet secretary must already have a close working relationship with the prime minister making the choice. Evidence of a close working relationship with a different senior politician (particularly a previous prime minister) amounts almost to a disqualification.

In the past, the long tenure of cabinet secretaries helped. In the first 100 years the job existed, it had only eleven occupants (for thirteen months after the end of 1961, all eleven were alive at the same time). Robin Butler was part of the fabric by the time Blair was elected; no one seriously tried

---

* Lord Heywood of Whitehall GCB CVO.

to disrupt his plan to retire on his sixtieth birthday. In the last few years, things have changed. Everyone at the centre knew that Theresa May would accept only Mark Sedwill when Jeremy Heywood retired due to ill health. But the absence of process meant that Mark was vulnerable when May was overthrown.

He lasted one year. When he left, Johnson gave him two pictures, portraits of Sir Francis Walsingham (England's first spymaster, a nod to Mark's origins in intelligence) and of Thomas Cromwell. King Henry VIII turned to Cromwell after the fall of Cardinal Wolsey, weighing him down with responsibilities and honours, until he regretted his over-dependence. Having made him both lord great chamberlain and Earl of Essex in April 1540, Henry had him arrested less than two months later. Cromwell was executed without trial on 28 July 1540. So, a farewell gift with a loaded backstory.

6

Problems Choosing Leaders (Particularly in the Civil Service)

The senior leaders I knew best were my fellow permanent secretaries. We met (nearly) every Wednesday morning in Conference Room A in the Cabinet Office. Up to forty people gathered around the hollow square table. In the middle of the hollow sits an older table, the table at which Charles II met his ministers. Behind the cabinet secretary's chair is George II's throne, roped off so that no one accidentally uses it. It's grand.

The forty characters changed regularly. Only three people who had been there when I started were still there when I finished. A few became friends. But most were simply good colleagues, people I was happy to work with but relaxed about never seeing outside work.

The cabinet secretary (Jeremy Heywood and latterly Mark Sedwill) was always in the chair, apart from when we met to discuss talent and succession planning, when we were divided into sub-committees. The first chair of my sub-committee was Nick Macpherson, permanent secretary at the Treasury.

When Nick gavelled us to order at the start of our first

talent meeting, he set out the single principle that would govern our decisions: potential. The sub-committees considered the claims of all directors general to promotion to permanent secretary. We placed all DGs in a nine-box grid. The best real estate was the top row, colleagues we felt had a better than 50% chance of promotion. The Stars ('ready now') were in the top right; High Potential ('ready in three to five years', in other words, needing more than one job before they would be ready) were in the top left, separated by Excellent, those who probably needed one more job to qualify themselves as serious candidates for a permanent secretary role. The middle right-hand box (Strong) was the next most desirable (if you wanted promotion), where your chances were less than 50% but you had one or two plausible target jobs. The bottom row was for colleagues, most often at the end of their Civil Service career, unlikely to be promoted further.

Nick emphasised that performance would not feature in our deliberations – plenty of DGs did a first-rate job but, for many reasons, were unlikely to progress further. The pyramid is sharply pointed at the top of the Civil Service. In the Home Civil Service, there are about 200 DGs and about twenty departmental permanent secretaries. The rest of the forty Wednesday Morning Colleagues (WMCs) head agencies or are permanent secretary-rank advisers. In the Diplomatic Service, there are about twenty-five DG-level jobs and usually two permanent secretary-level jobs (PUS and ambassador to the United States, though a second permanent secretary in London was added in 2022).

Over the years, I learned a lot about these leaders

from our discussions of future leaders. The most striking assumption, as we sat down, was that we were all very good at our jobs, not merely qualified but also best placed to assess our more junior colleagues. We behaved as if we were a circle of perfection.

Assuming ourselves to be perfect, we looked assiduously for candidates in our own image. We labelled such candidates the 'full package', DGs whose CV and temperament wholly qualified them to become permanent secretaries. Of all the odd ideas expressed in our talent meetings, this seems to me now the oddest. No one is the full package. For people to strive to be the full package or – worse – be told they are the full package is unhelpful and misleading.

The older I get the more slippery for me is the idea of intelligence. My dad attached importance to speed of comprehension; he used to say that one of his colleagues was just as intelligent as he was, he just needed twenty seconds more to understand something new. When Dominic Cummings worked in Downing Street, he said he wanted to recruit the brightest 'people who are a thousand times cleverer than I am'. He apparently meant people who could do things he admired and admitted he could not do himself, a skill set which, if measured by the number of premature resignations, proved ineffective in central government.

In the Foreign Office, the only exam results that feature in the HR paperwork are proficiency in foreign languages. The Office teaches over seventy languages and, having paid for the tuition, expects colleagues to pass exams, a requirement not always rigorously enforced. Looking at the pattern of postings over many years, it is clear that the

Foreign Office (at least subconsciously) recognises that excellence in acquiring foreign languages does not correlate closely with effectiveness as a diplomat. In the 2000s, the head of personnel at the Auswärtiges Amt told me that in the German Foreign Service the least reliable indicator for effectiveness as a senior diplomat was fluency in numerous languages.

By the time colleagues are DGs, no one is interested in how well they fared in university exams twenty or thirty years earlier. Early academic performance is not part of the voluminous paperwork. The ability to get things done is rated highly.

Without fully acknowledging our prejudices, we strove to be objective. To help us, we had plentiful paperwork. It was more or less useless. Everybody curates what is written down about them these days. Shortcomings were encoded so subtly that decrypting them was a hit-and-miss process. In the end I focused only on the CVs. What people had done and for how long was more useful than their self-assessment.

The biggest problem with the process was that no one acknowledged the spectre of patronage hanging over it. The chair was the single most important participant. The chair's preferences became clear to everyone else – to resist was to limit your influence in the rest of the discussion. After Nick's sub-committee had finished its work, the main committee considered the recommendations of all sub-committees. Where the chair of the main committee had a view, they could (and did) set aside recommendations. I tried not to do the same in committees I chaired. I did not always succeed.

We tend to forgive those who share our shortcomings. Permanent secretaries tend to be forceful characters, high performers demanding high performance from those around them. By definition they are doing important work, often under pressure. Subordinates are made aware of the pressure in some of their interactions with seniors. Put bluntly, the single thorniest issue that we failed honestly to tackle was bullying.

I have never met anyone who was a bully all the time. But I have never met anyone (except my dad) who seemed to me incapable of bullying behaviour when the stars lined up unfavourably. With Jeremy or Mark in the chair, and surrounded by professional equals, we all behaved impeccably; our behaviour in front of our boss did not so much as hint at the possibility of bullying in other contexts. But it was the elephant in the room.

We behave differently in different situations; we all compartmentalise our behaviour. When the Civil Service was failing to cope persuasively with allegations against Priti Patel, I was intrigued by the string of senior Conservative politicians attesting before microphones to the kindness of the home secretary. Just as with her Conservative Party colleagues, Ms Patel has always treated me with complete courtesy, but so what? The positive experience of 99% of your acquaintance in dealing with you does not invalidate the miserable experience of the 1%. One incident can have a devastating effect, even if the perpetrator forgets all about it or softens the details in their memory.

The inability to deal with senior bullies is not confined to the Civil Service, but the Civil Service is noisier than most employers about its zero-tolerance policy. So, it must do better. I suggest four components of a new approach.

First, those investigating and reaching conclusions must be separate from the Civil Service. One deterrent to civil servants lodging complaints is the history of senior colleagues closing ranks around one of their number who stands accused.

Related, departments need a staff counsellor, separate from the line management chain (the agencies and the FCDO have such a counsellor). Too many teams are too small and isolated for people to feel they can make a complaint or even seek advice without the risk of blowback.

Third, there needs to be a range of sanctions. Until 2022, one problem with accusations against ministers was that the only sanction (apart from criminal proceedings) was enforced resignation. Offences vary in intensity and severity – sanctions, too, need to vary. Otherwise, those sitting in judgement may find in favour of the defendant because they find the available sanctions too severe. A year without a bonus or pay rise, a cooling off period when promotion will not be considered, the withholding of an honour, and a requirement for training or mentoring could all be considered.

Fourth, there needs to be follow-up. Usually nothing happens after a case is closed. Even where behaviours fail to meet legal definitions, I have never known an accusation appear out of a clear blue sky. Pastoral aftercare for the accuser and accused should be part of the approach and the staff counsellor's responsibilities. Right now, accused parties who are cleared feel exonerated, even traduced. Having been told they have done nothing wrong, they feel no need to change their behaviour. Having failed to sustain their case, their subordinates feel they must knuckle down (or move) because the chances of successfully bringing a second case are slim. Everyone feels aggrieved and nothing improves.

The problem of the flawed genius exists alongside the problem of bullying behaviour. We make allowances for people who achieve outstanding results by unconventional means; sometimes the ends justify the means. In some discussions, there was almost a feeling that the flaw was an integral part of the genius and could not be separated, that in some way the colleague would have achieved less had they been held to the standards applied to everyone else. Norman Borlaug and Pablo Picasso were not civil servants; they are two of the few people active in my lifetime whose achievements might override appalling personal behaviour (not that Borlaug was badly behaved). None of the flawed geniuses in the Civil Service is doing anything of such quality and importance that their flaws can be overlooked.

The difficulties faced when choosing and developing senior leaders in the Civil Service are probably shared by other organisations. I noticed a general impatience to move up. The senior ranks of the Civil Service are chock-a-block with people who never did any job for very long – they agitate to move on and up quickly. When recruiters are sifting applications, the applicant's thirst for new and more senior work seems to trump the need to demonstrate sustained competence in their existing job. Apparent success must be banked professionally before its shortcomings come to light.

For a time, at the Ministry of Justice, the reorganisation of the Probation Service in 2014 looked like a shining success, bringing in twenty-one private companies to supervise over 150,000 low- and medium-risk offenders and saving shedloads of money.

By 2019, it was apparent the reorganisation had been an expensive disaster, whose remediation would take years and cost billions of pounds. But the most senior civil servants involved had moved on, promoted on the back of a signal 'success'. These days, only Chris Grayling (lord chancellor at the time) carries the can. He did indeed decide how to restructure the Probation Service but some of his errors were shared with the team, none of whom has ever suffered professionally for the flawed advice on which the lord chancellor based his decisions.

Ambition is a problem when assessing talent. Ambition is often regarded as an indicator of ability. Perhaps. But just as often ambition outstrips ability. My grandfather used to say that everyone gets one promotion too many – expressed another way, the Peter principle contends that, in a hierarchy, everyone rises to the level of their incompetence. Over the years, the colleagues prepared happily to say they were content with the level of seniority they had achieved were relatively few. The only person I heard say he was a 'bottom row of the talent grid' civil servant was already a permanent secretary (signalling that he would not run for the job of cabinet secretary).

So, ambition is a twofold problem. Most people do not know their professional limits. Senior jobs always attract a field of candidates, many of whose applications are easily set aside. Subsequent history (that is, the pattern of future applications) suggests that feedback is not clear enough.

Even when history suggests a job is frustrating or impossible to persuade others you are doing it competently, people apply if it is senior enough. Lyndon B. Johnson dismissed the vice-presidency as 'not worth a pail of warm piss', but he accepted Kennedy's offer to join him on the Democratic ticket in 1960 because of its proximity to the most powerful job in the world and the tantalising prospect of promotion to the job that counted. Civil servants feel similarly about certain thankless top jobs: being at the WMC table is the best place to campaign for the job you really want.

More problematic for the Civil Service is the reluctance of the best-qualified to apply for some of the most exposed senior jobs. Senior civil servants were always public figures but have recently become public targets, fit subjects for hostile media briefings by special advisers, in the same way as the political rivals of their bosses.

Problematic, too, is the reluctance of the modest, excellent civil servants who cannot imagine themselves in the top jobs and consequently do not push themselves forward. The self-promoters not only relentlessly push their own claims, but they also deter others from having a go.

Shuttling between meetings of WMCs and the FCO Board, I compared the dynamic of a group of which I was a member and a group I chaired. In the first, antipathy was clearer to me. In any group larger than two, it is likely that some members will not get on, at least some of the time. The antipathy may be hidden from the person in the chair but it is still there, potentially potent. In civilised company, we do not physically or often verbally attack each other but the undercurrents of hostility still swirl beneath the chairperson in their canoe.

WMCs was by far the larger group. In order to increase diversity, Gus O'Donnell* expanded the traditional meeting of permanent secretaries, who still meet occasionally, badged as heads of department. The head of department group is about twenty people. In Robin Butler's day, it was smaller because there were no Devolved Administrations to send representatives and the Ministry of Justice and Department for Digital, Culture, Media, and Sport had yet to break out of the Home Office.

A larger group is necessarily more unwieldy. In any large group, participants suspect that real decisions are taken elsewhere, in smaller settings where people can talk more freely. In the eighteenth and nineteenth centuries, and during the First and Second World Wars, the British cabinet was never larger than nineteen men. After the First World War, it grew and the Ministerial and Other Salaries Act (1975) set the number of cabinet minister salaries at twenty-one, plus the lord chancellor who is paid separately. Since then, the cabinet has never been smaller than twenty-two and usually larger, because one or two members are unpaid.

Since Gordon Brown became prime minister, cabinet meetings have generally been attended by over thirty ministers: full members, other members with automatic access granted by the prime minister (the chief whip, the chief secretary to the Treasury, the minister for universities),

---

* Lord O'Donnell GCB.

and ministers invited to attend when their subject is on the agenda (under Gordon, for example, the attorney general). When thirty people meet, especially when participants feel that speaking validates their presence, their meetings tend to be unsatisfactory. With so many contributions, a chairperson can sum up in the way they wish.

Large numbers also mean that everyone present doubts the confidentiality of proceedings. People leak with impunity from a large meeting. With a smartphone in silent mode, they can leak even while the meeting is in progress. Gordon Brown became so irritated with leaks that he asked his cabinet secretary to ensure cabinet colleagues surrendered their phones before entering the cabinet room. A large mahogany piece of furniture appeared in the vestibule next to the cabinet room, full of pigeonholes for ministers to deposit their mobile phones. At the first meeting in the phone-free era, participants were surprised to hear a familiar ring tone: Gus had forgotten to stash his own.

Despite the mahogany piece of furniture, leaking continues. I have heard more than one prime minister rail against disloyalty, in that moment forgetful of the leaking they had authorised before they were prime minister. Charles Kingsley invented Mrs DoAsYouWouldBeDoneBy in his book *The Water-Babies* – as good advice now as when written in 1862. Less well-remembered is Mrs BeDoneByAsYouDid. Those who have serially and blatantly undermined their bosses cannot be surprised when the same is done to them.

In the past, civil servants leaked less (and they still leak less than special advisers). It helped that they were not public figures – even the cabinet secretary worked in the background. These days, anonymity applies only to junior civil servants; when complying with freedom of information requests, only the names of colleagues who are not in the senior management structure are redacted. The requirement for civil servants not to answer back still holds good. When civil servants are attacked in the media, they rely on ministers, the cabinet secretary, and retired colleagues prominent enough to attract attention to spring to their defence.

In thirty-eight years, I only once felt stung enough to give my side of the story (after 'misspeaking' to the Foreign Affairs Select Committee in March 2020) but more colleagues want to get their version of events into the public domain and, having broken the rule once, feel less inhibited breaking it again. Ministers are sensitive to the change. They no longer assume that civil servants will be quietly loyal.

In the past everyone understood the idea of serial loyalty: for the time any civil servant worked for any minister, the civil servant would be loyal to their boss. That loyalty extended into the minister's and civil servant's retirement; what you did with a previous minister was discussed with successors as if the predecessor were in the room, circumspectly and respectfully. Everyone knew that civil servants' ultimate loyalty was to the Crown, and that they served the government of the day within the law. The ability to work wholeheartedly for whoever the British electorate returned to office was the defining feature of British civil servants.

In a way that simply did not apply in the past, ministers now look for civil servants personally loyal to them, including their permanent secretaries. Cabinet ministers insist on close involvement in the process of choosing their department's permanent secretary. Francis Maude sponsored the changes in the coalition government (2010–15). But for two years while I was PUS, there was an unbroken run of permanent secretary appointments made by secretaries of state who had moved on by the time the appointee actually arrived.

One of the signs of middle age is an increasing tendency to observe 'it used to be better'. On examination, the claims of any time to be a golden age are thin. But the fact that rows make their way inevitably and quickly into the media is a change for the worse.

Gus O'Donnell used to say that there should be more pictures hanging on the staircase in 10 Downing Street than outside the cabinet secretary's office in 70 Whitehall. (Cabinet secretaries as well as prime ministers put their photograph on the wall once they have left office.) David Lloyd George appointed Maurice Hankey as the first cabinet secretary when he became prime minister in December 1916. In the following eighty years, there were fifteen prime ministers and seven cabinet secretaries. Since Tony Blair became prime minister in 1997, there have been five prime ministers and seven cabinet secretaries. The assumption that a cabinet secretary was a fixture, a civil servant who had proven their mettle over a long career in public service, appointed by merit and willing and able to work for whoever the monarch asked to form a government has evaporated.

Maurice Hankey served for twenty-two years as cabinet secretary, working for five prime ministers: a Liberal (Lloyd

George), three Conservatives (Bonar Law, Baldwin, and Chamberlain), and one Labour, who also led a coalition government (MacDonald). His first six successors served for an average of ten years. Among them, only Robert Armstrong served a single prime minister, starting the year Margaret Thatcher became prime minister and staying eight years. Things changed after Tony Blair became prime minister in 1997. By 2016, I saw Jeremy Heywood, appointed by a Conservative prime minister, effectively put on probation by Theresa May and her team.

For twelve months, May's team put Jeremy through his paces. It looked like an extended interview, or loyalty test; it suited them to keep him dangling. They learned, perhaps more quickly than they let on, that he was their best option. Nobody could approach a policy challenge like Jeremy, rapidly make sense of it, and present compelling, practical responses. By the time Jeremy had secured his position, he was already suffering from the cancer that killed him.

The manner of Mark Sedwill's appointment (without process) and departure (after rowing with the next prime minister's chief adviser) has encouraged the idea that a cabinet secretary is the personal choice of a prime minister. The idea is of recent vintage but has taken root faster than Japanese knotweed. From Hankey to Butler, the convention around the choice of cabinet secretary had something in common with a pope emerging from the College of Cardinals. As an incumbent neared retirement, the field would quickly narrow, even though there was only one formal requirement for a cabinet secretary – that they should be a serving permanent secretary.

Over the years, three other criteria were informally added: the new boss should have deep knowledge of the money (to help prevent a prime minister from being bamboozled by the Treasury during spending rounds and budgets), deep knowledge of some aspects of domestic policy (which take up most of a prime minister's time), and be a plausible leader of 400,000 civil servants.

Each time a change was in the offing, the field as seen by senior civil servants was obvious, generally just two or three candidates. As with most jobs, more than one person at any time could fill it plausibly. When the race is close and one relationship is overwhelmingly important (the one with the prime minister), no one objected to the prime minister having the ultimate say. The prime minister always chose among the *papabile*. In 2018, no one disputed that Mark Sedwill was *papabile*; the problem was that appointment without process left him vulnerable when his patron left office.

In 2020, the Civil Service commissioner insisted on a proper process to choose Mark's successor. But the prime minister, more particularly the prime minister's chief adviser, leaned into the process even as the field was forming. The process was intricate and protracted but not independent – rather it was tailored to meet Dominic Cummings's interpretation of the prime minister's detailed preferences. Under the old system, Simon Case would not even have applied, a candidate with six months' experience at permanent secretary rank but who had never run a department would have failed the only formal requirement for the job. Dominic Cummings's keenness on Simon's candidacy explains why he was in the field and why he won the race.

With that personal history, a cabinet secretary has no independent power nor means to defend themselves if the prime minister, or (as importantly and more likely) the coterie around the prime minister, takes against them. How you leave a job is intimately connected with how you got the job in the first place.

The new vulnerability that applies to the cabinet secretary applies in spades to permanent secretaries. The convention that permanent secretaries served until they agreed with the cabinet secretary they should step down has gone, along with the retirement age. Their position rests principally on their relationship with their secretary of state; the idea of permanence persists only in their title.

When I became a permanent secretary, I spotted a difference between the advert to which I responded and my letter of appointment. The advert stated that the appointment was initially for five years with a further two years available by mutual agreement. The letter of appointment did not mention a time limit. The five years is part of Francis Maude's changes. Because the changes were made without a change in primary legislation, letters of appointment are the same as they always were. No one has bothered to challenge the term-limit in court. The idea of using the law to hang on when you are not wanted does not appeal.

In the old days, permanent secretaries had neither line managers nor annual appraisals. These days conversations with the line manager are more therapy than personal development, and the paperwork is heavy with implausible praise. But what counts are the unminuted conversations, between prime ministers and cabinet ministers, and then between the prime minister and their cabinet secretary: opaque, one-sided, and occasionally brutal.

Of course, there were poorly performing permanent secretaries in the past – the fact that no one assessed their performance helped them linger ineffectively in office. Earlier methods of tackling poor performance were too slow. But new ways of working are openly adversarial. If permanent secretaries are not seen to be the creature of their cabinet minister, they are vulnerable. And, being so close to the incumbent, they can be seen as suspect by successor cabinet ministers, even when the successor is from the same party.

All organisations have to identify and manage talent. In most organisations that is one of the duties of senior managers. But it seems to me that by putting the onus on the most senior we are perpetuating the faults in the system. In the end, it is difficult for anyone to find flaws in a system that has delivered that person to its top.

As PUS, I hankered after two changes, neither of which I was able to bring about: first, to professionalise the human resources function. For the first half of my career, the HR Directorate (previously known as Personnel Operations Department) was staffed exclusively by members of the Diplomatic Service doing a tour of duty before returning to standard diplomatic work. The rationale was that Foreign Office work was so different that only someone with practical, personal experience at home and in the field could be a credible personnel officer. Latterly, the HR Directorate is staffed with a mix of HR professionals, usually people who specialise in the public sector (and specifically Whitehall) and DS. Objectivity about those around us is as difficult as it is important: we have to try. But, in the end, I observed it was easier for colleagues removed from the fray, who were not thinking of their own return to the fray.

I discussed my second idea with Board members, who saw more clearly its problems than its merits, so the fact it went nowhere is probably fully justified. But it gnaws away at the back of my mind. I wanted to incorporate an element of peer review into talent management. The colleagues who see us most clearly are our peers and contemporaries. Each year, the Foreign Office takes in most of its new entrants in batches, who undertake induction training together. In my first year, the eighteen of us got together regularly for other training, including travel together (to Brussels, to learn about the EEC). Each cohort has a clear idea of itself.

I accepted the two most obvious shortcomings that my colleagues pointed out. First, not everyone joins by the most popular route, so not everyone belongs to a clear cohort. Those who join later or transfer from another part of Whitehall would be penalised. Secondly, part of the appeal of training in your cohort is that it is a wholly supportive group – people are not assessing each other or themselves against others. But, with work, I feel that the objections could be overcome, so peer assessment could be a useful input.

7

Constraints on Leaders

No matter how great the possibilities of their job, leaders are always aware of the constraints under which they work. They see obstacles strewn in the path of everything they are trying to achieve. Over time, they tend to become more cavalier in their approach to disposing of those obstacles.

Gordon Brown became prime minister on 27 June 2007. He had wanted the job ever since he went into politics and had been planning his initial actions in 10 Downing Street at least since Tony Blair's announcement on 7 September 2006 that he would step down within a year. First, he wanted to be surrounded by his people. As one of his Treasury team explained to me, 'Everyone and everything must be different. Not even the cat will survive the cull.'

Within twenty-four hours a new cabinet and new team of senior civil servants were in place. Even though Blair and Brown were from the same party, the change was as profound as when a new party and new leader are returned after a general election. (Boris Johnson adopted the same approach when he replaced Theresa May in 2019.)

Second, the new prime minister announced a new way of working. He had been particularly irked by the early

Order in Council which had allowed Blair's key aides to tell
civil servants what to do. The order, promulgated on Blair's
first day in Number 10, had allowed Jonathan Powell and
Alastair Campbell (both SpAds) to behave like ministers.
As my Treasury informant told me, 'For ten years, Ed Balls
was the second most powerful person in the Treasury and
managed that without instructing anybody to do anything.'
The Blair team's approach was felt to be antagonistic and
unnecessary.

The other immediate change made by Brown, which still
persists today, is the flying of the Union flag on UK government buildings every day. Previously, flags had flown only
on flag days designated by Buckingham Palace (generally,
royal birthdays and anniversaries, and feast days of the
four patron saints of the constituent nations of the United
Kingdom).

After the flurry of planned activity and congratulatory
phone calls, everyone waited expectantly for the roll-out of
Brown's master plan. It never came. Looking back, I think
it never came for three main reasons.

First, Gordon Brown's political philosophy did not
lend itself to being turned into a master plan. Although
he wrote (and read) more than any British prime minister
since Harold Macmillan, his books and pamphlets were a
mosaic of motivation rather than elements of a coherent
plan.

Second, even though they are powerful heads of government, wise prime ministers do not explore the limits of their
power, knowing it makes better sense to persuade others of
what they could do theoretically on their own authority;

they see the need for others to agree and implement their ideas. Throughout his time in Number 10, Gordon wanted to make a big speech about British identity in the twenty-first century, building on initial thoughts he had laid out as chancellor. But his own doubts and hesitations were magnified by everyone he spoke to; it stayed in the too-difficult tray.

And third, he was overwhelmed by events. Most people can fill their time at work to their satisfaction. British prime ministers can fill every moment with activity that other people think is vital and which they end up persuading themselves is vital. They end up neglecting their own agenda.

So, within days of taking office, Prime Minister Brown was up to his elbows in the crises of the hour, chairing Cobra meetings about a terror attack in Glasgow and unexploded bombs in London, dealing with floods in the north of England, and answering questions about everything under the sun in Parliament. The most obvious constraint leaders feel is time. Unless they are Louis XIV or Elizabeth II, they never have enough, and what they have is so frantically busy that they work in constant fear of departing the stage before achieving what they most wanted to do.

Leaders need to prioritise. If they do not, someone or something else will: their noisiest adviser or the noisiest issue in their in-tray will do it for them. The more senior the job, the easier it is to convince yourself that everything you are doing is important and necessary for you to do, and the easier it is to convince yourself that, without your personal input, any given issue will go awry. But the more senior the job, the more likely its incumbent will not be able to keep across every issue. The principal person to suffer in the failing effort is the job holder. You will spread yourself so thinly that no issue will get the attention the lead person on that issue needs to give it. You will work so hard that your health will suffer.

You must therefore prioritise and delegate. I have never met a leader who did not spout the importance of both in conversation. Very few leaders I have met have found it easy to prioritise or delegate in practice.

In the end a leader has no choice but to work through other people. The more important the job and the more overloaded the leader, the more scope those helpers have to push their agenda rather than their boss's. The rest of a government system works in awe of the head of government's office. Some of a leader's acolytes exploit that. When I worked for Jack Straw, I noticed the tendency of certain colleagues to include the words 'Number 10 wants' in their presentation, as if they had played the ace of trumps. Jack invariably asked, 'Who in Number 10? The building doesn't have a view.' Acolytes sometimes rely on the less attentive or more easily cowed not to double-check, confident that the prime minister too is not following a subject closely enough to contradict (or often even to discover) the policy being peddled in their name.

In Donald Trump's Administration, some of his advisers in the White House would combine the grandeur of their headed writing paper with the drama of a tight deadline to try to bounce through their hobby horse ideas. One senior official told me about the first time his department received a draft executive order (EO) at 9 p.m. on a Thursday with the instruction to clear it overnight, 'because the president wants to make the announcement tomorrow morning'. On behalf of his cabinet secretary, the official combed through the sixty pages of the draft, waking up colleagues for advice on the knottier, more technical, and most problematic sections. Come morning, he concluded that the draft EO's shortcomings were too glaring to be nodded through. He informed the White House that despite the president's keenness to proceed immediately, his department had major issues and would not be able to support it in its current form.

My friend waited for a rocket to explode from the West Wing. None was launched. He heard nothing further. But the next time he received a similarly adventurous proposal, he objected more confidently. By the end of the Administration, his initial response to out-of-hours unreasonable requests was to inform the White House that he would look at the papers in the morning.

Leaders must be careful choosing whom they allow to speak in their name. And they need to be aware that some speak in their name without ever being given that authority. That problem is especially acute for heads of government. The lustre of the building where they work misleads outsiders. The names of some buildings evoke the power of their occupant: in Foreign Office telegrams, the worldwide readership knows what an author means when they write about the White House, Élysée, Kanzleramt, or Kremlin. When an ambassador quotes a source working in any of these buildings, a reader assumes the source has the boss's ear.

In the UK, prime ministers traditionally accepted the help of civil servants whom they hardly knew, confident that they would work diligently for them because of the office they held. That is decreasingly the case. As the number of people working in Number 10 has grown, so has the proportion with a pre-existing relationship with the prime minister. Personal loyalty rather than professional competence has been driving appointments at the centre. The personal acolytes often know little about how government works. They carry a big stick, but they do not know how to wield it. They get frustrated, and their boss is more likely to side with his acolytes than the machine they cannot get to work. A Jeremy Heywood will always be able to get the machine to respond better than a Dominic Cummings.

Within the Civil Service, prime ministers' close collaborators shape their reputation as much as the prime ministers themselves. Perhaps inspired by the model of Malcolm Tucker, they often behave as if 'kicking ass' were the best way to get things done. Possibly. But I have never seen that approach work. Collaboration, courtesy, and humility attract and attach the people on whose work you depend. In the end, they spend a tiny proportion of their working lives in your presence, but those minutes affect how they behave the rest of the time. Micro-management, rudeness, and arrogance eventually screw up.

Part of the problem is that the cleverest advisers know that they have relatively little time to get things done. They therefore tend to be in a hurry. Revolutionary change tends to appeal to them more than incremental change, even if – throughout British history – incremental change has usually proved to be more long-lasting. The fact that, for most of the twentieth century, the two main British political parties were ideologically poles apart incentivised governments to attempt change so far-reaching that their opponents would not be able to undo it when they were returned to power. Sometimes the advisers feel the constraints more sharply than the boss. They know that advisers generally have less time than prime ministers to implement their agenda (and some have an agenda separate from their prime minister) because prime ministers rarely end their time in office with the same set of advisers that they had at the beginning.

So much information is now available that people tend to assume that all the relevant information is accessible, and they become impatient when leaders prevaricate. But comprehensive information is rarely available, and even more rarely is that information in comprehensible form. Crisis training exercises are designed to drive home that point. Scenarios give participants incomplete information, little time, and enormously consequential decisions to make. Exercises do not last long, but by the end everyone is exhausted and uncomfortably aware that real life could be just as vertiginously unfair.

People outside government often assume that governments have access to more information than they do. After all, governments have access to the product of three intelligence agencies whose work, by definition, is secret and so denied to the general public. In reality, the agencies' work is limited and specialised – relatively little of a government's work and decision-making is affected by them. In the past, the idea that the government knew more than any other player helped the government (including internationally); it meant an air of mystery hung over its work. The dispelling of that mystery in recent times is a further constraint upon them; people are less willing to give the benefit of the doubt when they share the same knowledge base.

Assumptions and reputations constrain leaders. No one has ever had complete control over their reputation, but in earlier times you could reasonably hope that how you worked and what you delivered would help shape your reputation. These days performance seems only tangentially relevant. For many politicians these days, particularly the most prominent, a section of the public has made up their minds no matter what they subsequently do. And the pre-existing opinion is much more likely to be negative than positive.

When a section of media comment is reliably, implacably hostile, you ignore it to survive. People hate being ignored. The relationship spirals down still further. Eventually, it seems, the critics forgive nothing, no matter how minor the consequences or the leader's personal involvement; they end up treating every mistake as malicious. More than in the past, leaders suffer an aggressive lack of sympathy on the part of some of the people they are trying to lead. In the UK, the simultaneous appearance of new media and Brexit has made this worse.

In the last century everyone got their news from the television or newspapers. Broadcasters were obliged to be politically neutral. Newspapers – mostly unapologetically – had a political party allegiance. If you inclined to Labour, you knew that the *Guardian* and *Daily Mirror* would be more congenial reading than the *Telegraph* and *Daily Express*. All organisations disseminating the news were legally obliged to get the facts right; if they failed, injured parties could take them to court.

This century, most people get their news from Facebook and Twitter. Anyone can wade in – no editor checks that facts are correct. Users share content that amuses or appals them. Extreme views attract more attention than moderate or balanced views. What is liked or retweeted is more likely to be recommended to others. Contributors can be anonymous, and anonymity permits shrillness, unkindness, and inaccuracy. Algorithms capture a user's developing preferences, steering the user to more extreme versions.

Brexit has divided the United Kingdom like no other issue in my lifetime. The division has deepened since the referendum. During the campaign, voters could be unsure, persuaded to some extent by arguments on both sides. In the polling booth, they had a single vote and had to come down on one side or the other. Someone who had been a '60% Brexiteer' was permanently categorised as a Brexiteer by his vote. Your voting intention determined where you looked for news. But none of the sources was for a '60% Brexiteer' or a '60% Remainer'. The sixty-percenters were encouraged towards and eventually corralled into the 100% end of the media market.

I follow a bunch of Remainers on Twitter. Their tweets are often entertaining, sometimes thought-provoking but always predictable. They hate Boris Johnson. They think he is cynical and self-serving, and that he adopted a strategically disastrous course for the country in order to further his personal ambition. They never, ever show understanding of, still less support for, the former prime minister. No matter what he does, they find fault or, at best, remain silent.

In Washington, I got to know Senator George Mitchell and his chief of staff, Martha Pope. Mitchell was President Clinton's Northern Ireland envoy and worked tirelessly and effectively to broker the Belfast/Good Friday Agreement. While serving in the Senate, he drove Martha to distraction by insisting, after every election, on an immediate visit to the county that had given him least support. He wanted to know why they had preferred his opponent in order to do better in the next election, six years ahead. In the new media landscape, why would politicians bother engaging with their opponents? New media algorithms curate what users read; revealed preferences are reinforced. Once the algorithm has worked out a user's political point of view that user is unlikely to be presented with information that might prompt them to reconsider.

The problem is bad for politicians in government but even worse for those in opposition. By definition their base is not large enough to elect them to national office. Growing the base was always a challenge (as Labour repeatedly learned in the 1980s). The new media have turned the challenge into the political equivalent of a mountaineer tackling Everest without oxygen.

Almost as soon as they are appointed, ministers become aware of the minor obstacles to achieving their agenda. They may be tempted to sidestep small rules whose rationale they do not understand or agree with. The longer they remain in office, the more burdensome and objectionable the small rules seem, rules that were written for other people who clearly needed to be restrained. But they are different. They can be trusted to be more responsible. They are wiser than the rule setters, who never imagined the set of circumstances now confronting leaders. So these new leaders toy with the idea of setting aside or temporarily suspending the rules. The defence secretary sits atop one of the most capable military forces in the world and yet cannot use those forces for anything, not the smallest or shortest deployment, without someone who knows far less than they do raising objections. Why should they put their plans to Parliament or even cabinet before the plans are implemented? Updates after the fact will suffice.

But the small rules are how the system ensures actions are legal and decision-makers can face those who will hold them accountable with confidence: they guard against caprice, they protect the bigger picture, and they peer uncertainly but determinedly at possible unforeseen consequences. They save waste and embarrassment, and they ensure that any enterprise is understood and supported by more than one person. Of course, they slow things down, which might mean that the ideal moment for action is missed. But in all circumstances, it is better to have explained and built support than to shoot from the hip.

As they relax and grow into office, leaders tend to forget that one day they will be out of office. They forget that the rules they find most annoying are the ones they would most wish to constrain their opponents with when it is their turn to sit behind the ministerial desk. Before proposing any change, they should ask themselves how they would feel if people who did not share their worldview benefited from the change.

Ignoring the rules is often associated with corruption, enriching or otherwise benefiting the leader or their circle. As such, such behaviour is easy to categorise as 'always wrong'. I have come across one exception, but in the end I think it is the exception that proves the rule, rather than undermines it.

In the Knesset, Theodor Herzl's portrait hangs behind the Speaker's Chair because Herzl was the visionary who first dreamt up *Der Judenstaat*, but it was David Ben-Gurion more than anyone else who was responsible for turning that dream into reality. Ben-Gurion was Israel's first prime minister. His whole life was sublimated into the Zionist cause, to establish and then secure a state for the Jewish people in the Biblical lands of the Levant. Because he was present at the creation, he was responsible for writing many of the laws and rules of the fledgling state.

But, for Ben-Gurion, the cause was greater than the rule book. To attract a new investor, to secure the practical backing of a powerful new supporter, Ben-Gurion would bend any public procurement or tendering rule. The country was the beneficiary, never himself. When he was dying, Israelis walked in silence along the street in Tel Aviv where he lived and the traffic stopped, so as not to disturb his fitful sleep. He was the greatest Israeli. But when he died, he had almost nothing to leave his three children. His work, including his bending of the rules, had all been to benefit the state rather than himself and his family.

Corruption is wrong, but the fact that occasionally it might be justified poses a challenge. With such rare examples in mind, a leader may be tempted to dismiss those accusing them of corruption, ill will, or ignorance: critics fail to see that the public need was too urgent to follow the rules. Perhaps. But, when bending the rules, a leader needs in that moment to think how they would justify themselves to those disadvantaged by the rule-bending. Ben-Gurion knew exactly what he was doing and why, and he was open and honest; he did not pretend he was not breaking the rules. His first thought when breaking the rules was how to explain himself to his critics. But Israel's need was so sharp and the benefits so clear that opponents understood and lived with the rule-breaking. A leader's corruption may only possibly be justified if they are prepared to subject themselves to scrutiny. Otherwise, the idea that they should be exonerated because they know their rule-breaking serves the public good even though no one else agrees is merely beguiling rubbish.

In the UK, conventions are as important as laws and rules. In a country (the only country apart from Israel) without a constitution written down in one place, conventions are a key part of governance. Because not everything is written down, good governance depends on political leaders knowing how to behave. Peter Hennessy calls this the 'good chap' theory of government. It is not that British political leaders are inherently good – it is that they know what constitutes good behaviour.

Before the nineteenth century, British leaders were often related to each other (the 'cousinocracy'). Everyone who mattered was related to a large group of people who also mattered. Even as the ruling class grew, British leaders continued to go to the same few boarding schools and the same two universities well into the twentieth century: Rishi Sunak is the forty-first prime minister (of fifty-seven) who was a pupil at a public school (thirty-three went to Eton, Harrow, or Westminster School); forty-four prime ministers studied at Oxbridge. As well as acquiring their education at public school and old universities, they acquired a sense of how things were done.

This sense of how things were done pervaded the greatest institutions of the British state: Parliament and the law. But, crucially, these institutions were open to new talent. Such was the confidence of those running these institutions over the centuries that they never bothered to keep them closed: they were institutions for the brightest and the best men. Generally, the brightest and the best would be found in the existing ruling class but outsiders, if they were smart enough, were welcome. The best-remembered prime ministers of the nineteenth century – Peel, Gladstone, and Disraeli – were all sons of self-made men, as were the greatest jurists: Tenterden, Denman, and Romilly.

As the Tory/Whig, Conservative/Liberal duopoly collapsed in the first half of the twentieth century, the establishment – starting with the king – worried about the behaviour and agenda of the new socialists. But Parliament thoroughly schooled new arrivals before they reached the top. King George V got on well with Ramsay MacDonald and George VI got on even better with Clement Attlee. Queen Elizabeth II was famously close to Harold Wilson.

It turned out that socialists were happy to work within the existing framework; conventions were respected.

Until Tony Blair's election, Labour governments were strikingly more restrained in the creation of peerages. Mac-Donald never nominated more than thirteen in one year, and Attlee never more than twenty-six (in 1946, when – after his landslide victory the previous year – he was enacting the most far-reaching parts of the Labour manifesto). Both led administrations that coped effectively with an Upper House with a large Conservative majority. The passing of the Life Peerages Act in 1958 foreshortened the consequences for the legislature of the creation of a peerage, and the mass clear-out of hereditary peers in 1999 created more space in the House of Lords. The Blair government anticipated the new state of affairs by nominating eighty-seven peers in 1997 (still the record for a single year).

To function well, the British system needs the person atop it not merely to apply convention but to be conspicuously sympathetic with it. The UK's socialist prime ministers have understood that, at least instinctively. Iconoclastic leaders of older political parties have posed a greater challenge. Asquith and Lloyd George were George V's most difficult prime ministers: the former wrung out of him a private pre-election promise to create 100 new Liberal peers should the House of Lords defy a re-elected Liberal government; the latter sold peerages to swell the coffers of his party.

The royal prerogative underpins the British system. Over centuries, its exercise has transferred from the monarch to the prime minister. Since the Constitutional Reform and Governance Act passed in 2010, almost nothing is left to the monarch's personal discretion. Although the monarch maintains the right to be consulted on its exercise (indeed her signature is still required for many things to happen), she cannot block or even impede the prime minister. A disrespectful prime minister can only be endured, and outlasted.

No rules govern the size of the House of Lords, and only flimsy convention suggests who might or might not be appointed. Aware that its bloated size was difficult to defend, the House supported Dan Byles's private member's bill allowing lords to retire and Terry Burns's report in 2017 recommending a system of 'two out, one in' with the objective of steadily reducing the number of members of the House to 600 (to make it smaller than the elected House). In the first six years since the House of Lords Reform Act (2014) was passed, over 130 peers have resigned, but 190 new peers have been created. Membership of the House remains over 800.

Since Robert Walpole was George I's prime minister, monarchs have accepted their prime minister's recommendations; disputes have taken place behind closed doors. Because there are no rules, this part of any prime minister's patronage has always been controversial, and every prime minister has made scandalous nominations. The House of Lords Appointments Commission (established in 2000) vets nominations for propriety, but its conclusions are merely advisory. Prime ministers would enhance their own reputation if they followed the Commission's advice.

These days public appointments are made on merit, with the notable exception of ministers. Even when political parties have tied their leader's hands and chosen their shadow cabinet for them, the membership accepts that, the prime minister having accepted the monarch's invitation to form a government, they have a free hand. No one has ever suggested that the resulting ministry is composed of the best qualified or most competent. Prime ministers reward allies, balance factions, develop talent, and stymie rivals. The cabinet is an unarguably partisan part of the system, but the system includes appointments whose independence from government is essential to their function (the judiciary, the church, regulators) and others who need to be able to work with governments of any political stripe, so closeness to a particular prime minister may later prove problematic (the Civil Service, the military). Prime ministers can skew the processes that precede recommendations for appointment, but the system will break down if they do; if an appointee's only legitimacy is closeness to an incumbent PM, that appointee will be ripe for removal the moment that PM disappears.

In an already centralised system, Number 10 is accreting more power. By convention, many appointments in the public sector are cleared by the prime minister. What started as a courtesy – to inform the prime minster before a public announcement – has changed. Where once the prime minister was informed, now they must approve. What started as a check became the power of veto, which in turn grew into the power actively to shape selection panels and shortlists. This power has grown almost invisibly over the twentieth century. Until the 1960s, cabinet ministers selected their own junior ministers. Now a secretary of state accepts the prime minister's choice of their junior colleagues without (publicised) demur.

Diplomatic Service appointments are still formally the responsibility of the foreign secretary. Prime ministers – and their staff – used to interest themselves only in who represented us in Washington and in political appointees. For all my career, the number of political appointees was never more than two. When Patrick was PUS, the number was zero, as it was during the Cameron/Clegg coalition (easier than agreeing a split between Conservative and Liberal Democrat nominees). The HR director used to tip off successful candidates after the foreign secretary had signed off their appointment, the final two stages (clearance by the prime minister and approval by the monarch) being formalities. No more. These days, nominations can be overturned by Number 10.

Britons have only a passing interest in their constitution, which can be summarised in a single sentence: 'Parliament may do whatever it likes.' That state of affairs grew gradually over centuries, with large strides forward in the middle of the seventeenth century (when Parliament ordered the execution of Charles I, the last of thirty-five English and Scottish kings to die a violent death), the end of the seventeenth century (when Parliament invited William of Orange to displace James II), and the beginning of the eighteenth century (when Parliament fixed the succession for the childless Anne on a remote German cousin, who was merely seventieth in line by custom). Each of these strides saw significant powers transfer from the monarch to Parliament or – more particularly – to the chief (latterly prime) minister supported by Parliament.

When the party of which the prime minister is leader enjoys a healthy majority in the Commons, they can ignore or treat with contempt the body on which their power depends. These days, a British prime minister enjoys powers of patronage and policy-making more complete than in the dreams of Charles I. The fact that those powers depend utterly on the continued support of the House of Commons means they are not absolute, so the British public does not appear unduly alarmed. They know that when the ruling party has no reliable majority, the prime minister is weak, as Jim Callaghan showed in the late 1970s and Theresa May after the general election of 2017. But, in my time, Thatcher, Blair, and Johnson all enjoyed periods of power that an eighteenth-century tsar would have recognised.

The completeness of their power can tempt them to be careless of convention. Going to war is the most serious decision a government ever takes. Even though the Conservative opposition under Iain Duncan Smith was enthusiastically supportive of the Iraq War, the parliamentary Labour Party was not, so Parliament was kept at bay until hours before hostilities began in March 2003. When Johnson sensed he lacked a majority in Parliament to crash out of the EU without a deal in October 2019, he attempted to prorogue Parliament to prevent it acting on its unhappiness with his decision. The most important conventions, it turns out, can be made justiciable, although it is the essence of royal prerogative that it is not generally justiciable.

Attracting less publicity, other, lower-profile conventions are decaying. In 2019, senior figures around Boris Johnson asked habitually, 'Is it against the law or just against convention?' If the answer was the latter, then they proceeded with confidence. In the end, no one has the power to make a prime minister respect convention.

Checks and balances are not written into the British constitution in the way they are into America's, but for centuries prime ministers have respected the independence of other parts of the British system, even when involved in key appointments in those sectors: the judiciary, the military, the Civil Service, the BBC, the Church, regulators, and academia. These days, that independence is under attack. Parts of the system that have relied on the good sense and good behaviour of the person at the top and their team are finding it difficult to defend themselves. Publicity sometimes helps. Boris Johnson found it impossible to persuade panels to select his first preferred candidate to be chair of Ofcom (Office of Communications). Public and Parliament need to be equally vigilant about the chairpersonship of the Board of the Judicial Appointments Commission. In the legal year beginning 1 October 2022, the Commission will process 1,200 judicial appointments. Because the process to replace Ajay Kakkar as chair sputtered into life only three months before he was due to step down on 30 September, he agreed to stay until the end of the year.

The business of government is tough. It is difficult to hold the public's attention, so governments resort to slogans and repetition, and then become defined by those sound bites. Tony Blair said that, just at the point when he was physically sick with repeating a message, the public had probably just begun to hear it. The history of effective repetition in politics is an ancient one. In the second century BC, Cato the Elder is said to have ended every speech he made in the Roman Senate: 'Carthago delenda est' ('Carthage must be destroyed'). He was an effective warmonger, encouraging the Republic to embark on the Third Punic War.

The only time I had heard of Tony Blair before he became leader of the Labour Party was an approving comment of his philosophy as shadow home secretary: 'Tough on crime; tough on the causes of crime.' Campaigning to win his first general election, he explained his top three priorities as: 'Education, education, education.' Nothing he said (as opposed to did) as prime minister resonated as widely. Which is probably just as well: slogans are better suited to campaigning than to governing. Looking at how he governed, his slogan should have been: 'Improved Health, Peace in Northern Ireland, Solidarity with the United States.' Specificity as well as brevity makes a slogan memorable. And being too specific when governing is likely to lead to disappointment: a slogan can be hung like an albatross around the politician's neck. Slogans grab attention and then they constrain.

A last constraint on leaders is human frailty, their own and other people's. At some point, everyone will let a leader down, including leaders themselves. They will have a bad day, make a wrong call, or be distracted by something of overwhelming personal interest but of merely passing interest to their team.

I have listed some of the constraints on leaders, the most important I felt or observed myself. I have more sympathy with some than others. I have most sympathy for leaders suffering the constraints (often a lack of resources) that make their job more difficult to do or make it more difficult for the people they are trying to lead to understand what they are doing (often a need for confidentiality). I have less sympathy for leaders trying to dispense with necessary constraints, the constraints that ensure transparency and accountability, that protect an institution from the caprice of a transient leader. Constraints that remind leaders they are not masters of the universe are a good thing.

8

The End of Leadership

Leaders who die in office are either monarchs, dictators, or struck down too early. But lifelong leadership is rare these days – even Pope Benedict XVI decided to step down from a job that, before him, had seen only one voluntary resignation in 2,000 years. Leadership ends more quickly than most leaders are prepared for. At the peak of her powers and prime of her life, C. J. Cregg snaps, 'You think I'm not aware that I'm living the first line of my obituary right now?' in season seven of *The West Wing*. A long retirement is now the norm, and most leaders at some point during their leadership become uncomfortably aware of the fact.

Among top leaders, almost no one knows when to go. High office is intoxicating. The longer you occupy it, generally the more comfortable you become and the more expert at pulling the levers of power. And the more aware you become of just how much you could accomplish with a little more time. Everyone understands what Elizabeth I meant when on her deathbed she whispered, 'All my possessions for a moment of time', but leaders know best of all.

Refusing to name a retirement date helps to maintain energy. Knowing you are in the last six months of a job, you might be tempted to take your foot off the gas, or your colleagues – especially when not entirely convinced by your decisions or agenda – might be tempted to wait until your successor is in harness. One reason junior ministers in Britain tend to be weak and ineffective is that no one thinks they will be around for long. In the first twenty years of the twenty-first century, Britain had seventeen different ministers for energy. Cabinet ministers are precarious enough (ten culture secretaries since 2010), but junior ministers' security of tenure is worse: their average incumbency this century has been eighteen months.

Until 2011, civil servants in the UK knew when they would retire: the day before their sixtieth birthday. Other male public sector workers retired at sixty-five and female workers at sixty. Exceptions were rare and individually negotiated. Age discrimination laws put paid to the brutal clarity of a fixed retirement date.

By the time I was appointed PUS, permanent secretaries had a five-year contract, renewable by mutual agreement for a further two years. Initially, I wanted to serve until my sixtieth birthday (the magical day on which I would have earned a full pension). As the years rolled by, I wanted to serve until the government had consolidated overseas policy-making into one ministry. The possibility of consolidation ebbed and flowed. The creation of the Department for Exiting the European Union (DExEU) and the Department for International Trade (DIT) in 2016 marked low tide. At the beginning of 2020, the FCO received a bigger portion of the expiring DExEU than the dowry given at its creation. In the following six months, the plan (discussed with Boris

Johnson when he was foreign secretary) to recombine FCO and the Department for International Development (DFID) came to quiet fruition.

I wanted to serve for the first year in the new ministry, the year of the unavoidable disagreeable decisions that accompany any merger. But, as the cabinet secretary explained to me, I was to be Moses, not Joshua, seeing and certain of the promised land but not entering it. My last day was 1 September 2020, the last day of the FCO.

In the private sector, many leaders are time-bound by contracts. But term limits are the exception among political leaders. The Twenty-second Amendment to the US Constitution limits the president to two four-year terms in office. In Costa Rica, presidents cannot succeed themselves. In post-Communist Russia, presidents had to stand aside after two terms but could offer themselves for re-election after their successor had served a single term. Until Putin, on the international stage Russia was strikingly rule-abiding; domestically, even Putin has assiduously applied the rules with relation to his own position. He placed a puppet in the Kremlin, whose strings he pulled from the Russian White House, for the single term the rules required him to wait before running again for the presidency. While he was prime minister and Medvedev was president, Muscovites joked that everyone in Moscow was either a Putin man or a Medvedev man, 'except for Medvedev, who's not quite sure'. It turned out that Medvedev was a Putin man, his supporters merely hoping in the face of mounting evidence that he might be more independent.

In 2014, Russian constitutional lawyers claimed that

the annexation of Crimea reset Putin's electoral clock: the change in the country's size meant, in effect, the creation of a new Russia – Putin was entitled to two new consecutive terms in the new Russia. Eventually, Putin tired of relying on legal chicanery or working through a puppet. In 2020, he had the law changed to align with reality: he can now serve as long as he likes. Authoritarian countries, including those that stage elections whose result is never in doubt, are not democracies. The acid test is the relevance of the ballot. In democracies, the electorate decides at the ballot box when they have had enough.

Few democratic leaders step down voluntarily before the electorate has had enough. Involuntary exit was one reason Enoch Powell said, 'All political careers, unless cut off in mid-stream, end in failure.' Even when the electorate plays no role, departure is ignominious: palpable ill health drove Churchill and Macmillan from office; the early, easier-to-disguise-in-public stages of dementia caused Wilson to resign.

Having won the 2015 general election, David Cameron boasted in private that he would be the first leader of the Conservative Party since Stanley Baldwin to choose the time of his going – even leaders apparently at the peak of their power cannot peer very far into the future.

The looming prospect of retirement affects leaders' behaviour in office. They try to stave off the evil day, some by ignoring it and others by designing stratagems to delay the day. Most pick up pace as the exit gets closer. And they nearly all try to fix their succession, in an effort to secure their legacy.

Nearly every leader I have worked with has had an awkward relationship with their successor. Historically, this awkwardness cast a long forward shadow: most monarchs had an awkward relationship with their heir, who, after ascending the throne, strove to be different, no matter the qualities others saw in their predecessor. The only recent exception in British history was George VI and Princess Elizabeth.

Unlike monarchs, prime ministers and presidents generally do not know who their successor will be. Even when there is a high degree of presumption (which may be justified by events), there are no guarantees. For most of the time Winston Churchill was prime minister, Anthony Eden was seen as, and was widely referred to as, the crown prince. Churchill hung on, through a change in monarch and bouts of ill health, which became more severe and more difficult to disguise, in the hope that someone else would turn up.

Clement Attlee felt similarly about his crown prince: for most of the twenty years Attlee was leader of the Labour Party, Herbert Morrison was seen as his most likely successor. Attlee stayed on long enough, even fighting the 1955 general election when he was seventy-two years old, to see his parliamentary party discount Morrison on grounds of age. Although he was five years younger than Attlee, they felt that, at sixty-seven, Morrison was too old to embark on a new career as leader.

Churchill's heir presumptive was more than twenty-two years younger than Churchill. Although Eden suffered poor health as early as in his twenties (stomach ulcer) and had major surgery when he was foreign secretary (for gallstones and for complications arising from the original operation to remove the gallstones), he was robust enough to outwait Churchill. Within two years of taking over, he fully justified his old boss's hesitation about his temperament for the top job.

Tony Blair was another prime minister who doubted the suitability of his obvious successor. With three election victories under his belt, and with an agenda only partially realised, he was reluctant to hand power to Gordon Brown. Even after telling the Labour Party conference in September 2006 that he was addressing them for the last time as leader, he continued to behave as if he had years ahead of him in office. In early 2007, he instigated a comprehensive policy review. As Iraq Director in the Foreign Office, I was swept up in this work. Even at the time, it felt otherworldly, an implausible attempt to bind his successor to Blair's priorities. The work disappeared into Whitehall's wastepaper baskets the moment Gordon took over.

At the last minute, Blair also cast around, not particularly subtly, for an alternative successor. He had observed that the Labour Party was leery of potential leaders who had flunked their moment. One reason why he had been ahead of Brown in polls of the party membership from the moment John Smith died was that Brown had been the alternative to Smith three years earlier. At the time, and ever since, Brown has stressed that personal loyalty meant he could never have opposed his old mentor. Alternatively, Brown could be said to have bottled it.

Blair's choice was David Miliband. When Brown inevitably got wind of the plot, he bought David off with the offer of the Foreign Office. David's hesitation came back to haunt him three years later, when the membership preferred his younger brother as Brown's successor as Labour leader.

The last British prime minister successfully to hand-pick his successor was Harold Macmillan. From his hospital bed, he orchestrated the takeover of Alec Douglas-Home to the astonishment of everyone who did not know of Macmillan's distrust of Rab Butler, popularly seen as his natural successor. Inviting a person to form a government is part of the royal prerogative. In the 1960s, the queen still had some discretion, which in this case the outgoing prime minister was happy to exercise on her behalf.

Unhappy with the over-mighty part played by someone departing the political stage, the Conservative Party rewrote its rules for deciding its leadership (or rather decided formally how this should be done for the first time – previously leaders had reliably 'emerged' from the parliamentary party pack). Since then it has always been clear who, in any of the leading parties, the monarch should call (even if it was not immediately clear in 2010 which party leader should be given first chance to form a government).

Mrs Thatcher was more successful than Tony Blair at stymying her presumed successor. Michael Heseltine took himself to the back benches, as the Westland affair reached its climax in 1986. From then, he was explicitly the anti-Thatcher alternative. After her cabinet had explained to her the impossibility of retaining the Conservative Party leadership, having failed to secure re-election in the first-round ballot in October 1990, Thatcher bowed out, throwing her support to her chancellor of the Exchequer as the person most likely to block Heseltine. Grooming a replacement had never been on her agenda; in an unpromising field, she picked the apparently most Thatcherite candidate, who prevailed, but subsequently John Major endured a scratchy relationship with his patron, as she realised that his priorities were not hers.

A reluctance to prepare a successor or even a plausible slate of possible successors is not exclusive to the top of British politics. Internationally, the vice presidency of the United States has proved a reliable stepping stone to the top job, and then because of its constitutional position ('a heartbeat away from the presidency') rather than enthusiastic planning on the part of any president. Of the fourteen men to serve as president since the Second World War, six had previously been vice president.

Many leaders are not merely reluctant to prepare a successor but also take active steps to prevent a rival from emerging prematurely. The most extreme historical model is the Ottoman Empire. When a new sultan was enthroned in the Sublime Porte, he routinely arranged the execution of his failed rivals. The lack of immediate alternatives helped him establish his rule. In Germany, Angela Merkel did something similar (admittedly non-lethal) after assuming the chancellorship in 2005.

Early in her tenure, *Spiegel* published an analysis of the nine people most likely to succeed her. It alerted her to possible sources of danger. One of the nine named told me later that in the years after the article appeared, Merkel systematically moved, derailed, or defanged all nine. The consequence was that, when she was serious about retirement, having won her fourth term as chancellor in 2017, her party scratched about unconvincingly trying to find a successor. The first choice (Merkel's preference) crashed and burned without ever facing the electorate. The second choice suffered the same fate after leading the CDU to its worst ever federal election result. Friedrich Merz, one of the nine, succeeded only at the third time of asking; he must now rebuild the CDU rather than lead it into a fifth consecutive term in government.

Tiberius, as imagined by Robert Graves, offers a beguiling approach to succession planning. Nearing the end of the second longest reign of any Roman emperor, Tiberius must have been aware that his reign had been in every way worse than Augustus's. Among his family, he chose the only heir guaranteed to make a worse fist of the job than he had done: Caligula, an inbred twenty-four-year-old, was already displaying the insanity that would cause him to kill his sister (impregnated by him) and appoint his favourite horse (Incitatus) as priest and consul. According to Graves, the stratagem worked: posterity viewed Tiberius more favourably than his successor.

Gus O'Donnell used to bemoan Clive Woodward's approach to securing a legacy. Under Woodward, England won the Rugby Union World Cup in 2003 for the first time. It was a huge and hugely popular achievement. Having lifted the Webb Ellis Cup and secured his knighthood, Woodward resigned. The problem for English rugby was that he had designed a system that only he could understand and lead; a system dependent on one man failed English rugby for the next decade.

Under Gus, the Civil Service decided that all departments should have a succession plan, updated every year. The plan would name one 'if the serving perm sec fell under a bus' candidate – someone qualified to take over immediately, at least for an interim period, and possibly as substantive successor. The plan would also list at least three other candidates who would be ready (or needed to be helped now in order to be ready) to compete when the incumbent permanent secretary was due to stand down.

Gus was right: leaders need to plan at least the barebones of their succession. Departure cannot be avoided by not thinking about it, so better to think about it than hope it will (or will not) turn out all right without your intervention. Leaders generally want to be remembered positively; that legacy cannot be secured by a weak or badly prepared successor. In the end, it is in a leader's interest to have a succession plan.

Throughout history, royal crown princes have had a wretched time. However cosy their relationship with their father, at some point they are waiting for daddy to die. In politics, crown princes fare even worse, always heir presumptive, never heir apparent, with a position protected in law and custom. So, a leader should prepare a field of candidates rather than groom a single favourite.

In helping to assemble a field, leaders in the West should recognise that they will not have the final say. Steve Jobs could handpick Tim Cook because Steve Jobs was the founder and major shareholder of Apple. Boris Yeltsin could designate Vladimir Putin because Russia after the collapse of the Soviet Union remained more autocratic than democratic.

Institutions that want to remain healthy should take steps to protect themselves from the prejudices and enthusiasms of any given leader. The statutes of Christ's College, Cambridge, granted in 1506, repeatedly stress that a serving master must be excluded from the process to elect his successor. Every time a new chief of the defence staff must be selected, the British military learns the meaning of civilian control. A serving CDS's effort to load the dice in favour of their preferred candidate generally results in someone else getting the job.

In helping to develop a field, a leader should aim for variety and resist the temptation to find a clone. Those appointing your replacement will probably be looking for a contrast in style. After seventeen years of the hyperactive ministry of Geoffrey Fisher, Harold Macmillan decided the Church of England needed respite when he recommended the appointment of the more contemplative Michael Ramsey as archbishop of Canterbury: 'Enough of Martha, time now for Mary.'

Ensure your possible successors have plausible CVs. In any organisation, there are springboard jobs: higher profile – and, frankly, more important to the organisation than others at the same level – jobs that if done well indicate that their holder is capable of work higher up. Leaders need to take care that these developmental jobs are filled by younger colleagues with the greatest potential, and then guide these younger colleagues as they make their way up the organisation.

In the FCO, experience in the foreign secretary's and PUS's offices was the surest indicator for who would eventually become a senior ambassador, Board member, and PUS. Since 1982, three out of ten PUSs have worked in the foreign secretary's private office and four have been private secretary to a PUS. All bar one were senior ambassadors immediately before becoming PUS.

The competition that preceded my appointment as PUS included every knight in the Diplomatic Service who had not announced he was in his final job. And no one else. Five white, straight 'Sirs'. It was easy to resolve that next time would be different. When my retirement was announced, six colleagues stepped forward. From a diverse field, a white knight was appointed (he was the best candidate) but the Foreign Office was moving in the right direction.

As I look ahead, the field is already taking shape for three years' time. I predict that three-quarters of shortlisted candidates will be women: the quartet will be the best four (senior) people working for the Foreign Office. They are all colleagues who have served on the Board of the Foreign Office (three as directors general); all senior ambassadors, that is to say, SMS3, which means leading one of the top twenty overseas posts; all with at least twenty-five years' experience of diplomacy and development; all candidates capable of leading (I would add, inspiring) a worldwide service of nearly 20,000 people. Serious. Tested. Expert. Adaptable. Confidence-inspiring.

Leadership ends but life goes on. In my experience, 'What next?' does not preoccupy many heads of government: their efforts focus on extending their leadership for as long as possible. Which is one reason why most former leaders I know look rather bereft in retirement.

Their foundations attract satisfactorily large donations; their speeches command six-figure fees; they continue to fly by private jet. But their books achieve more impressive advances than sales and, too soon, they find themselves seeking a platform rather than platforms seeking them. Among western leaders, Jimmy Carter seems to me to have managed retirement the best. He was young (fifty-six) when he failed to win a second term as president – the need to do something else was obvious and urgent. The Carter Center filled a gap, as democracy advanced in Latin America and Africa. And the Nobel Peace Prize is the ultimate validation of a public life well spent.

One thing every political leader I knew in office and later in retirement has in common is that they are all nicer in retirement. Some, who seemed to take satisfaction in fuelling a reputation for stone-hearted bastardry in office, turned into pussycats. They all have more time and show more interest in things that are not at the top of their agenda. It's almost as if, in office, they thought politeness wasted time or betrayed weakness. For whatever reason, all of them are more pleasant to talk to when it's over.

9

The Good Leader

The definition of a strong institution is one that can withstand a period of poor leadership. Successful institutions need to be flexible enough to survive abuse (sometimes conscious, sometimes unwitting) at the hands of those trying to run them. But long-term survival depends on replacing a poor leader as quickly as possible; in the end, healthy institutions need good leaders. I have been mulling the attributes of good leadership all my adult life. Before putting finger to keyboard, I know that what follows will strike some as a blueprint for Frankenstein's monster, weird and otherworldly, as unattainable as it is undesirable.

Undaunted, I begin with authenticity. You will not persuade anyone to follow you for long if you are not clear in your own head about who you are. Too often, spontaneity is seen as synonymous with authenticity: although it is a marker, it is not the same thing. A lack of spontaneity indicates a possible problem with authenticity. A lack of spontaneity suggests too much control and a fear of saying the wrong thing. I see this in media interviews all the time. Political leaders who I know to be clever, funny, and passionate come across as narrow, timid, and lacklustre. In front of a microphone, their media training is the most obvious thing about them.

Nobody is allowed to say 'yes' or 'no' in reply to a question, even when their subsequent answer can accurately be summarised as 'yes' or 'no'. Almost no one is confident enough to crack a joke or make a mistake. The exception is the prime minister. Only when you are the biggest boss can your misspeaking be transformed into new policy or breezily disowned.

Authenticity does not mean continually spilling your guts in public – discretion and discipline are allowed. But, when you speak, you do not say anything you believe to be untrue; you do not feign enthusiasm you do not feel; and you do not pretend to be someone you are not.

A key part of authenticity is recognising you cannot be a leader all the time. When Nicholas Soames asked his grandfather if it were true that he was the greatest man alive, he could not conceive of his mother's dozing father as a statesman and Nobel laureate. No one can embody all good qualities, all the time, and no one can appeal to everyone in the same way. Even sanctity drives some people to distraction: Germaine Greer could not abide Mother Teresa, whom she encountered in the first-class cabin of a long-haul flight. Authenticity requires the recognition of shortcomings and determination to overcome those shortcomings.

Good leaders admit their flaws and do something about them. By the time they are leading, they cannot do much to change the fundamentals of their character, but they can mitigate them. They can have people around them who are allowed to take them aside for a quiet word, to create space for them to eat or rest or exercise. The best 'mistress' figures do this. When Gordon Brown was being his most difficult, Sue Nye was able to clear the room and talk like a friend, offering bananas and Kit Kats and five minutes' time out.

Even more important is choosing a team whose strengths complement your weaknesses, and then acting on their advice and empowering them to do the things you cannot do or do not have time to do, and then backing them when things do not go according to plan and giving them credit when they do.

Good leaders let their teams know what they most care about, and share what's on top of their mind – not everything (too much sharing is creepy) – but those things that others need to know in order to make sense of their approach and priorities.

In five years as PUS, I shared just two personal stories, about my brother and my father. My brother was gay: funny, perceptive, generous, flamboyant, unapologetic, and hounded because of all of the above. He was diagnosed as HIV-positive in April 1987 and died on 14 October the same year. I think about him every day; I miss him. But I also think about what he suffered, about how prejudice and presumption can add to suffering. Wilful lack of sympathy and understanding makes other people's lives worse.

My dad suffered from Parkinson's for many years. He diagnosed himself a couple of years before doctors agreed, when he was about seventy years old. He loved his family and he loved his summers in France, and he continued to enjoy both to the full until he was eighty. But a year or so later his condition deteriorated; with his balance shot to pieces, he fell frequently and hurt himself. Just before his eighty-second birthday, he went into a nursing home where he died a year later. His final weeks were sad, and a bit uplifting. His family gathered around his bed, reconciled with each other (at least for a time) and said goodbye.

Work carried on under the shadow of my dad's final illness. I continued to deal with the full spectrum of foreign policy, from Afghanistan and Brexit to Yemen and Zimbabwe. But colleagues knowing that something else was going on in my head was a help in dealing with everything at work.

The good leader does not fit a template. But, having watched others lead, I see a range of attitudes and behaviours that make it more likely that a leader will be good. Before plunging further in, I make three general observations.

I have never seen a leader at work at any level who everyone has agreed was a good leader. Equally, I have never seen a leader who had no followers. Sometimes I suspect that the presence of followers is validation for leaders, proof that they are doing a creditable job. But it is the most unreliable kind of validation. All leaders have advantages they can confer on members of their team. No matter how miserable generally a leader's performance, some acolytes will find personal benefit in sticking close. In politics, those who are there at the finish do best in the Resignation Honours List. A leader should from time to time examine the motivation even of their closest followers.

Leaders never completely escape admiration for the system that delivered them to its highest perch. By definition they will think that a system that benefited them could not be all bad. Reforming from the top in the UK has always been slow. Every time a party enjoys a huge parliamentary majority, it behaves as if the majority will persist. The Labour Party, although in government for less time than the Conservatives since the Second World War (thirty years), won the three largest majorities in the House of Commons (1945, 1997, and 2001). Its leaders talked about the inbuilt advantages for the Conservatives, but each time they had the chance they failed to address them.

Reforming the fundamentals spooks potential reformers. Success over time protects whatever has been successful. Temporary custodians of that success are wise to hesitate before messing with an alchemy they do not completely understand. In the US, Republican abuse of Senate procedure to block or delay Democratic presidential nominees to the Supreme Court drove Democrats wild. In particular, Republicans exploited the filibuster: in the Senate, you need sixty (out of a total of 100) votes to end debate ('cloture'); because Democrats could never muster sixty votes, Republicans were able to keep debate going until Democrats gave up the idea of a final vote ('filibuster'). Over recent decades, Democrats tended to be in the majority in the Senate, but they hesitated to change the rules because they knew new rules would be permanent and their majority was not. In 2013, the Democratic majority leader finally pushed through a limited modification of the filibuster to prevent the minority blocking future nominations to the Supreme Court. Within four years, Trump was in the White House and Republicans in the majority in the Senate. Democrats found themselves unable to prevent the appointment of conservatives Brett Kavanaugh (in 2018) and Amy Coney Barrett (in 2020) to replace liberal justices Kennedy and Ginsburg. The lesson is 'take care' rather than 'don't try'.

No matter how good a leader is, their style will never suit everyone. One of the puzzles of political commentary through the ages is commentators' assumption that their low opinion of any given leader will be universally shared. In the past, editors had the chance to balance views expressed in their newspapers, seeking and showcasing different perspectives. They could temper the dodgy enthusiasms of their columnists. New media are not subject to any moderating or editorial influence, and followers choose whom to follow. They are not obliged to dilute their preferences by seeking alternative points of view. Leaders are aware that their chances of converting opponents or even of making them pause to reflect on their opposition are now vanishingly small. So, leaders double-down; leaders in power think they can focus without penalty on their base.

Second, you cannot know in advance who will be good, still less who will be very good. Leaders take time to hit their stride. They have to hope that their early (and, on reflection, avoidable) mistakes are either small enough or invisible enough not to fix a negative view in the minds of their team. At the beginning of his second term as prime minister, Tony Blair mused in private about getting away with numerous small errors of inexperience, relieved that they had not been spotted or, at least, not stored up and used against him.

Third, people used to think that pedigree counted. Your class determined your suitability to lead. In the eighteenth and nineteenth centuries, the House of Hanover chose all its brides and grooms from German royal houses. They did not have to govern a large territory – Saxe-Coburg was 217 square miles – they just had to be Protestant and royal. Queen Victoria frowned on brides from major royal houses: too grand. King George V changed established practice to allow marriage to British commoners only in 1917 – the fact that the UK had been fighting most source countries of royal brides for three years was relevant. Until 2013, descendants of George II needed the monarch's permission if they wanted to marry legally and maintain their position in the line of succession; the Succession to the Crown Act (2013) restricted the requirement to the first six people in line to the throne.

In the UK, pedigree mattered to more than the House of Hanover. In the eighteenth century, the cousinocracy provided the country with most of its prime ministers. More prime ministers sat in the House of Lords than in the House of Commons until the twentieth century. Even then, Winston Churchill (prime minister until 1955) was the grandson of the 7th Duke of Marlborough. The last aristocrat prime minister left office only in 1964: the 14th Earl of Home had to renounce his peerage to get the job but was able to return to the House of Lords in 1975 as Lord Home of the Hirsel.

Disquiet at the commercially tinged backgrounds of prime ministers Peel, Gladstone, and Disraeli did not stop their political rise nor prevent them from being effective in office. From the start the powers that be were confident of the wish of the interlopers to fit in. The prospect of the first

Labour prime ministers in the first half of the twentieth century was much more unsettling. But, however radical the prospect, both Ramsay MacDonald and Clement Attlee turned into pillars of the establishment in practice. An early death deprived MacDonald of the conventional honours in retirement, but Attlee scooped the pot. As he wrote of himself in a limerick for his brother in 1956:

> There were few who thought him a starter.
> Many who thought themselves smarter.
> But he ended PM,
> CH and OM,
> An Earl and a knight of the Garter.

The unconscious genius of the British ruling class was its permeability. Newcomers were welcome, if they supported the Crown and Parliament and believed in the superiority of British institutions and the British way of life. Over the nineteenth century, the statute book caught up with a religious tolerance already widely displayed in society. Barriers to Roman Catholics and Jews were removed. It helped the Catholics that several of the grandest noble families had never given up their religious allegiance to Rome. The ruling class was confident enough to be flexible and unthreatened by outsiders who wanted to become insiders.

The British ruling class had always been open to able newcomers: in the sixteenth century, Wolsey, Cromwell, and Cecil all rose to be the second most powerful person in England, despite their humble birth. But the nineteenth century saw the dethroning of pedigree as the key attribute of leadership. In parallel, universities began to value and reward intellectual rigour. It turned out that personal competence rather than blue blood was more useful when trying to lead. The empire played a part. The British may (according to J. R. Seeley) have acquired an empire 'in a fit of absence of mind' but, having acquired it, they strove purposefully to keep and exploit it. To do that, they needed a class of administrator willing and able to leave the UK. Young men with more ambition than wealth staffed the empire. What they learned in the colonies was repatriated: administrative reforms that were embraced mid-century in the UK started in the colonies. Sir Charles Trevelyan started his professional life in Calcutta before writing, with Stafford Northcote, the report that transformed the Civil Service into a merit-based institution. The Foreign Office held out for fifty years after the publication of the North-cote–Trevelyan report in 1854, but British reforms were always piecemeal rather than comprehensive.

Personal qualities, rather than qualities that an individual might be assumed to possess because of the class he or she belongs to, are now key. Application forms no longer ask what an applicant's father did for a living or for family connections to, say, the university where the applicant is seeking a place. It has taken a long time, such a long time that people have lost sight of the transition, but leadership is now about personal ability, hard work, and gumption rather than family or class.

My personal take on historical changes in British leadership aired, and caveats stated, what makes a good leader now?

Effective leaders are different. Isaiah Berlin thought leaders are:

> wiser, not more knowledgeable ... their vision is more 'profound', they see something the others fail to see; they see the way the world goes, what goes with what, and what never will be brought together; they see what can be and what cannot; how men live and to what ends, what they do and suffer, and how and why they act.

To be all of that effectively is to be a good leader.

I was a civil servant, which might explain why I prize how a leader constructs their team. Leadership is a team sport. No matter how few people are remembered later, every leader who is remembered was supported by a team. Lack of wider knowledge of the team does not mean it was not there or was merely incidental to the leader's success. As Brecht observed: 'Young Alexander conquered India. He alone? Caesar beat the Gauls. Was there not even a cook in his army?' Effective leaders remember they lead a team effort, even if posterity forgets.

Apart from leaders at the very top, most leaders insert themselves into an existing team. As they start, an awareness of what went before, of the fact that the team functioned before their arrival, will help. The leader is like the conductor of an orchestra: if they're lucky the orchestra will already be good but, however good or bad, taking time to get to know them, to make clear that your success depends on them, will help. As a child, I saw a black-and-white film called *Raising the Wind* (written by the man who scored the early *Carry On...* movies) about a group of aspiring musicians. At the climax, the students apply for a scholarship; the application process requires them to conduct the Sinfonia of London. The hero (Leslie Phillips) arrives on the podium with a stumble and a gag at his own expense, which endears him to the orchestra. He wins enough of their affection before he raises his baton to coax from them a passable performance of Rimsky-Korsakov and a round of applause. The twit (Kenneth Williams) treats the Sinfonia players as dimwits, instructing them precisely how to play almost every bar. Nettled, they seek further nit-picking clarifications before delivering a super-fast rendition of the *William Tell* overture and a raspberry to Williams on departure.

How leaders pick their team, what they allow their team to do in their name, and their relationship with team members in adversity are key tests. Patronage is real. It can be delegated but it does not disappear. The human resources process, especially when convoluted or protracted, can disguise the existence of patronage but does not erase it. At the end of the process, one person makes the decision, either explicitly or, more often these days, by chairing the meeting that agrees the appointment. Where leaders bestow their patronage is a key test of the quality of their leadership. Good leaders are surrounded by good people, appointed to complement, even to challenge, the leader rather than to cheerlead. Good leaders do not feel threatened by having members of their team who are better than them at aspects of the job.

When you are tired, out of the office, and out of touch

with latest developments, when you are on the phone, asking, 'Should I come back?' you want your team to tell you what you need to hear rather than sit silently at the other end of the line or tell you what you want to hear. If you do not have that relationship with your team, you are not a good leader.

The single most effective head of government whose work I witnessed at close quarters was Angela Merkel. At the beginning of her chancellorship, she inherited Gerhard Schröder's team in the Chancellery, a building with more open spaces than people. The politicians moved out immediately with their defeated boss, but the civil servants stayed for a time to help manage the transition.

In my view, the strongest civil services are politically neutral, their members accumulating experience and expertise over many years serving governments of whatever complexion the electorate chooses (I declare an interest as a retired British permanent secretary). Their personal political affiliation is irrelevant to the job they do; it is one of the few topics out of bounds for conversation with their political bosses. In Germany, the civil service is a profession where members are permitted not only to belong to political parties (also allowed in the UK) but also publicly to avow their party affiliation and campaign in elections.

When looking to fill the top jobs in their departments, German ministers generally appoint members of their own party. Because the Auswärtiges Amt was continually occupied by FDP ministers for three decades at the end of the twentieth century, German diplomats disproportionately embraced liberalism. Those who unabashedly carried a candle for the Greens and SPD came into their own when, first, Joschka Fischer and then Frank-Walter Steinmeier became foreign minister.

The most senior opportunities for diplomats belonging to the CDU/CSU were in the Chancellery. Merkel chose Christoph Heusgen to be her foreign policy adviser shortly after she assumed office. He was one of the Four Musketeers (my label, which they liked): the senior civil service advisers dealing with aspects of overseas policy. The others were Jens Weidmann (economics), Uwe Corsepius (Europe), and Ulrich Wilhelm (spokesperson). Whenever she travelled abroad or entertained a foreign leader in Berlin, Merkel was invariably accompanied by this quartet. In her sixteen years as chancellor, each of these four key jobs was occupied by only two men; Corsepius served twice, with Nikolaus Meyer-Landrut taking his place for the four years he was secretary-general of the European Council in Brussels. In 2011, Steffen Seibert (ex-ZDF newsreader) replaced Wilhelm, when he went off to run ARD in Bavaria. In 2012, Lars-Hendrik Röller replaced Weidmann, when he became president of the Bundesbank. Heusgen served the longest, becoming Germany's ambassador to the United Nations in 2017, when he was succeeded by Jan Hecker.

The group had Merkel's confidence and they had her back. They served her loyally and energetically. They were all among the very best in their field, chosen for their competence more than their political affiliation (but not denying the importance of political compatibility). They had clear and separate areas of responsibility. From outside, they appeared to work in harmony, even though it was just as clear that they never became personal friends. They did not always agree but they never briefed against each other, and they never leaked. Merkel's expectations of them were clear from the start and they never let her down.

At different points, all eight men had moments of professional difficulty. Merkel backed them. She did not exploit their screw-ups. They apologised and everyone moved on. Again, the relationships were steely, professional – until the end, they addressed each other with the formal 'Sie' rather than the familiar 'du'. Merkel attended Heusgen's sixtieth birthday in his favourite restaurant (Olivia and I were also there). She was the unavoidable centre of attention, but she did not stay long – just long enough to be the good boss celebrating a landmark with one of her senior team. Boundaries were clear and accepted. The media appeared to respect the group's solidarity. They did not try to drive wedges because they knew it would not work.

Floating above the praetorian guard was Beate Baumann, a legendary and almost-invisible-to-the-outside-world figure in Merkel's Chancellery. She had been with Merkel the longest, the only colleague permitted to call her boss 'Frau Merkel' rather than 'Frau Bundeskanzlerin' like everyone else. She was the conductor of Merkel's orchestra. And she stuck to her lane and let everyone else get on with their job. In five years in Berlin, I saw her only once, flitting out of the office when David Cameron arrived for lunch. Leaders need top advisers who are selfless, who do not need their own public profile and who do not secretly hanker to displace the boss. Baumann perfectly filled that key role for Merkel.

I saw something similar in Washington in the presidential campaign of 1996. I watched Senator Bob Dole claw his way to the Republican nomination through the gymnasia of Iowa and town halls of New Hampshire. When his candidacy was foundering, he defiantly stepped down as Majority Leader in the Senate; he wanted to be president and he did not want anyone to think he had a fall-back plan. But that moment came relatively late in the campaign – he had already secured the delegates he needed to be his party's nominee. Until that point, he had been travelling the country and relying on his team in Washington to keep the Senate ticking over.

In this vital task he was helped by his veteran chief of staff. Sheila Burke started working for Dole in 1977 as a health policy expert. She was appointed Dole's top staffer on the Finance Committee when he became chair in 1981, simultaneously beginning a master's in public administration at the Kennedy School of Government. In 1985, she became his deputy chief of staff when he became leader of the Republicans in the Senate, stepping up to the top slot the following year. Everyone in Washington knew that she spoke with her boss's voice, reliably interpreting her absent boss's priorities. Whatever she said would not later be overturned by Dole. Whenever she was not confident that her boss would agree, she deferred a decision until after she had managed to consult him. Her confident knowledge of her boss's mind meant business in the Senate did not grind to a halt.

Busy leaders need helpers who can represent them when they cannot be there and take decisions in their absence.

Colleagues will speak in their name whether they like it or not. The words 'Number 10 wants...' may not impress Jack Straw, but they provide iron guidance for most officials outside Number 10. Leaders need to take care who they allow to speak in their name. Merkel and Dole chose so well that their choice enhanced their own reputation.

Private secretaries are oil in the machinery of government. They increase their bosses' capacity; they follow up when their bosses are distracted; they are sounding boards and human shock absorbers. In the past, they were anonymous; now they join their bosses in the firing line. Often they are criticised for failing to prevent a course of action objectionable to the critic. Private secretaries can magnify their bosses' shortcomings but more often, in my experience, they take off the rough edges. In Disney's *Sleeping Beauty*, three good fairies bestow christening gifts on Princess Aurora. Flora and Fauna have already blessed the baby with song and beauty when Maleficent interrupts proceedings. The wicked fairy curses the girl to prick her finger on a spindle before sunset on her sixteenth birthday and die. Merryweather is unable completely to undo the evil, but she softens the child's fate: Aurora will fall into a deep sleep rather than perish. Private secretaries are sometimes cast in the role of the good fairy Merryweather, blunting the excesses of their bosses. Good private secretaries help their bosses become better leaders.

Leaders should never forget they lead people, not machines. That starts with their immediate team: 'Whose plans will be disrupted if I decide to work this weekend? Is my plan important enough to justify that disruption? If "yes", how can I help them cope with the disruption?' Curiosity in and care for the people immediately around them indicates leaders might have the necessary curiosity in and care for people further afield. At the height of the Falklands War, Mrs Thatcher discovered that the PUS's wife was in hospital for cancer treatment; she sent Anne Acland a large bunch of roses from Chequers, with a handwritten note promising 'the scent of flowers from an English country garden for you'. Thirty years later, Antony told Mrs Thatcher's biographer (Charles Moore) how grateful he had been for the gesture.

As a prime minister paws over statistics or the ORBAT (order of battle), they cannot be paralysed by the thought of the human beings represented by the numbers, but they must not forget them. Near the start of the Falklands War, on 4 May 1982, an Argentinian Exocet sank HMS *Sheffield*, the first loss of a Royal Navy ship since the end of the Second World War. Twenty sailors were killed that day. After the defence secretary had broken the news to the House of Commons late that evening, Mrs Thatcher sat in her Commons room, with the home secretary, in tears. When Whitelaw left, he told her detective not to allow anyone in; she wanted to be alone. If you feel the disagreeable human consequences of your decisions, you are more likely to take good decisions.

Good leaders behave well. In recent British history, the template is Lord Carrington. He had just resigned when I joined the Foreign Office, but his positive example lingered over the department all the time I worked there. Carrington was polite to everyone. His courtesy did not vary, whether he was talking to a president or a cleaner. He listened. Even decades later, those who worked closely with him recalled their time with him with a smile and a catch in the throat. He took an interest in everyone around him. At his funeral, his son recalled an incident when a senior official in London determined that his father had to be informed of some development in the middle of the night in Egypt, where he happened to be visiting. Carrington was more solicitous for the welfare of the team dispatched to inform him than interested in the content of the message (which did not, in his view, justify the kerfuffle). No one could ever tell whether he was having a tough day, because he never visited his frustrations on anyone else. No one feared to tell him what he needed to know, because they knew their reception would be respectful. He never shot the messenger, and even new messengers knew that.

Too many leaders appear to model themselves on Dr Jekyll and Mr Hyde, simpering in front of people they want to impress and snarling at people whose good opinion they feel they do not need, unaware of the transformation. When confronted, they look mystified, even offended. And yet everyone knows when they are raising their voice, or swearing, or slamming a door, or throwing a piece of furniture. It is not difficult to compile a list of behaviour that is never acceptable and not difficult to abide by it.

Most leaders I worked with were polite most of the time, but few were polite all the time. Because they lead, their flashes of annoyance are remembered by and become a problem for those around them, even if they never work that out. When you are busy, you are not aware of what you are not being told, of those around you holding back – not aware until, perhaps, it is too late.

The most consistent leader I have seen at work was the queen. In the middle of her first-ever overseas visit, she set out her approach to public service in a six-minute speech broadcast on her twenty-first birthday. Princess Elizabeth was in Cape Town, accompanying her parents on a three-month tour of southern Africa. Sitting alone in a hotel garden, she dedicated her whole life – 'whether it be long or short' – to the service of the United Kingdom and the Commonwealth. The language was simple and clear. She set herself a standard by which she could subsequently be judged. At the end of her life, the consensus overwhelmingly agreed she had met that standard.

In a constitutional monarchy, the monarch's functions are apparently marginal, except when they are not. All the powers that used to be the prerogative of the sovereign have moved slowly and irresistibly to the prime minister. Their remaining powers are in the most delicate part of the country's governance. They must invite a member of Parliament to form a government in their name. Usually, after an election or an internal government putsch, the choice is clear. But in 2010 it was not. The system swings into action guided by one cardinal principle: not to embarrass the monarch. The fact that, throughout fraught and private negotiations, everyone knew the monarch was there, symbolising continuity and the expectation that, however thorny, the immediate political knots would be untied, was essential comfort to the country.

Most weeks, the prime minister has a private audience

with the sovereign. No one else is present. The PM's principal private secretary sits in an outer office with the sovereign's private secretary getting through their own agenda. The audience fulfils at least three functions. First, it is a chance for a prime minister to explain what is going on. During Elizabeth II's reign, the knowledge that they would have to account for themselves to a person who had served in the armed forces in the Second World War and who had lived through every domestic and international crisis for over seventy years concentrated the mind of the prime minister. Under any monarch, they always have at the back of their mind the need to explain their actions to their sovereign.

Second, the rarest event in a prime minister's official life is a conversation unbriefed to the media. Everything prime ministers say tends to find its way into the public domain. They might be able to talk to a spouse or sibling without fearing that the conversation will appear later in the *Daily Mail*, but family members, however loyal and supportive, are usually not very knowledgeable about politics. Queen Elizabeth II was the ultimate discreet and well-informed audience. Conversations between monarch and prime minister are never minuted. Convention requires everyone who meets the monarch to respect the confidence of their conversation. Even foreign leaders feel bound by that convention.

Third, as the journalist Walter Bagehot summarised, the monarch's rights at the top of the UK system are: to be consulted by, and to encourage and to warn, their prime minister. In conversations with Elizabeth II, she was not merely a sympathetic ear, she could share the benefit of her

experience. Her first prime minister was Winston Churchill. She met more than one quarter of all US presidents,
indeed almost every world leader of note after ascending
the throne in 1952.

For the country as a whole, the monarch fulfils other
essential functions. At a time of drama or crisis, they are
a rallying point, a connection with our past, a proof that
even greater difficulty can be overcome. As Covid swept
the UK and the world in the spring of 2020, over twenty-
six million Britons listened to the queen's broadcast on 5
April. The subsequent reaction was international. The post
bag at Buckingham Palace heaved with messages of thanks
from around the world.

In a fragmented political, media, and cultural landscape,
Queen Elizabeth II cut through. She was the most famous
woman in the world. Every leader wanted to meet her. In
2018, the UK staged the largest ever Commonwealth Heads
of Government Meeting. Forty-seven heads of state and
government converged on London, at the time the largest
gathering of heads of state and government ever seen in the
UK. Most were explicitly clear that the reason they came
was to see Her Majesty at what was expected to be the last
CHOGM where she personally presided (because she had
stopped travelling internationally in 2015, and the UK hosts
CHOGM on average once every twenty years).

I saw the personal impact of the queen when I was
permanent under-secretary. One of my duties was to be
present in Buckingham Palace when new ambassadors and
high commissioners presented their letters of credence.
The queen received more credentials than any other person

in history, partly because she reigned for so long (and this is explicitly a task for a head of state) and partly because most countries only became independent countries able to post ambassadors during her reign. In previous times, when ceremonies were rarer, the foreign secretary used to be present, the PUS deputising when the foreign secretary was not available. When foreign secretaries began travelling more, the PUS became the permanent replacement.

The hundred-plus ceremonies I took part in were all different, but they all had something essential in common. No business was transacted, no matter how determined the new ambassador was. But a tone was set. Every ambassador was treated with the same warmth and dignity, no matter the size of the sending state or the sometimes-fraught state of the bilateral relationship. Conversation was wide-ranging and tailored to the guest. Spouses (present from the outset) and members of the embassy or high commission (admitted towards the end of the ceremony) were included in the conversation. At the end, everyone left happy. Happiness is an underestimated component in international relations. People who feel respected and welcomed by their hosts are more likely to work hard to promote the relationship.

Nobody knew exactly what the queen thought about anything, but everyone expected her to do the right thing, to find the right words or to make the right gesture. And, in seventy years, she did not disappoint.

Good leaders display grace. President Obama made his first overseas trip as president in April 2009. After attending the G20 Summit in London, he flew to Strasbourg for the NATO Summit. To celebrate NATO's sixtieth anniversary,

President Sarkozy and Chancellor Merkel symbolically hosted the Summit in Strasbourg and Kehl, border towns standing opposite each other on the Rhine. As with most joint Franco-German gestures, the French got the lion's share of the action, Strasbourg being eight times larger than its neighbour. But the Germans were determined to make their own splash, so leaders flew to Baden-Baden, which offered a more stylish backdrop for dinner on the first evening.

Because NATO membership was already at twenty-eight, space in the dining room was limited; heads of delegation were accompanied by just one official. I sat behind Gordon Brown. NATO seats delegations alphabetically by country name in English. So Gordon sat next to Barack Obama and I sat next to General Jim Jones, the new national security adviser. For three hours leaders gave their prepared remarks. The most memorable were Berlusconi's (because he told an off-colour joke) and Juncker's. The prime minister of Luxembourg was already the longest-serving head of government at the table, which felt like his justification for the otherwise unaccountable length of his intervention. Obama listened inscrutably. Smarting on his behalf, I silently calculated that the US matched Luxembourg's total annual expenditure on defence in less time than dinner was taking: $0.22 billion compared with $705 billion per year. In his remarks, Obama betrayed no irritation. He stuck to his script, welcoming the leaders of Albania and Croatia to their first Summit and reconfirming America's defence commitment to Europe. His first outing on the European stage cemented his position as the most popular US president in Europe since Kennedy.

Leaders from powerful countries start with an inbuilt advantage in international meetings. No matter how paltry their personal qualities, the audience always pays attention. Arthur Balfour served for longer in the British cabinet than any other minister: twenty-seven years (one year longer than Churchill) including three years as prime minister and three as foreign secretary. He owed his rapid rise in politics to his uncle, Robert Salisbury, the prime minister who first appointed him to ministerial office. Salisbury's actions when he retired were a dictionary definition of 'nepotism': he urged Edward VII to invite his nephew to form the next ministry (allegedly the origin of the phrase 'Bob's your uncle' for unwarranted good fortune). In office, Balfour neither said nor did anything memorable but in international meetings other participants hung on his every word: even the bland command attention when they represent the most powerful country in the world.

Good leaders are self-aware; they know their limits; they recognise that other people's ideas can be better than their own; they do not impose their will just because they can. Just as no one is good at everything, no leader is adept at all aspects of leadership. And they know it. Humility is the single most attractive feature in a leader.

Good leaders are good communicators. Historically, this is a recent requirement. Shakespeare put into the mouths of medieval kings speeches for which there is no evidence in the historic record. Queen Elizabeth I gave a rousing address at Tilbury, which only troops within a hundred feet of the monarch declaiming from her horse might have heard. Parliament was the venue of the earliest great British political speeches. Proceedings began to be published in 1771; Thomas Curson Hansard began printing transcriptions of parliamentary proceedings in 1809 (though transcriptions of parliamentary proceedings were not comprehensive until 1909). The need to persuade voters grew with successive reforms to the franchise in the nineteenth century. Politicians at the end of the century had to be able to command the attention of huge gatherings; Gladstone apparently managed the feat for hours at a time.

PUSs in the FCO remained remote figures until the second half of the twentieth century. Officers joining in the 1940s and '50s neither saw nor heard anything of Sir William Strang or Sir Ivone Kirkpatrick, who remained hidden in their corner office on the ground floor of Downing Street West. On 1 December 1973, Sir Thomas Brimelow began writing a secret letter once per month to heads of mission. Because the letter was sent by diplomatic bag, its contents were often out-of-date by the time they reached much of the readership. The Secret and Personal Letters, as they were known, were the one category of work that PUSs were allowed to consult in retirement, before the Freedom of Information Act dispensed with most of the strictures of the thirty-year rule. John Coles replaced the letter with a fortnightly telegram, which John Kerr continued until a damaging leak. Recently, PUSs have communicated with the worldwide team via blogs and tweets, responding personally to comments posted underneath what they have written.

Tony Blair was the best communicator I saw in Number 10. Whether talking to a handful of colleagues at a farewell party or the massed ranks of the Labour Party at a conference, or doorstepped unexpectedly by a microphone-wielding journalist, he always seemed to have the right words. Despite being written by someone else (with Alastair Campbell most often credited), he managed to make other people's words his own. Gordon Brown also spoke pithily but never looked happy, the delivery of his comms blunting their effectiveness; you lose half your audience when you look miserable.

The contemporary stress on the ability to communicate underlines the fact that most people have only superficial contact with a prime minister. If they meet, they meet fleetingly in a controlled setting. They know their leader primarily from television appearances (the bedlam of PMQs and more sedate set-piece interviews and political broadcasts) and secondarily from written pieces. Tony Blair acted at Oxford and was a barrister before he became a politician; Boris Johnson was a journalist before his election as MP for Henley. Politicians with a background in comms tend to communicate better.

The advent of twenty-four-hour news channels has increased the pressure on prime ministers to communicate constantly. Over my career, the threshold over which an event required official comment dropped steadily. Confronted by developments that seemed to him too minor to require reaction on the record, Alec Douglas-Home would occasionally ask his private secretaries, 'Do we have to say anything at all?' When he was chancellor, Helmut Kohl would disappear from public view for up to a fortnight at a time (sometimes associated with his annual 'cure' to shed weight). These days, leaders' press offices would not allow their principal to slip from view for so long. No event is too small to escape the need for prime ministerial comment – saying anything, it seems, is more important than saying something substantial.

The mania for saying something is related to the mania for action. These days leaders behave as if perpetual motion were part of their job description. In my twenties, I read the Palliser novels. At some dramatic moment in Trollope's recreation of Victorian politics, the powers-that-be required an unambitious prime minister to quieten things down. Plantagenet Palliser was their choice: a wealthy duke who had nothing to prove. He jibbed at enforced inactivity, objecting to the idea of being in office but not in power. Those who had placed him in the highest office reminded him of his dependence on them and prevailed upon him to play the part they had assigned him. Activity is not the same as achievement; statements are a meagre form of activity. Sometimes inactivity is the most beneficial policy option.

Good leaders pace themselves. Patrick once told me the story of an attempt at upward management by Pierson Dixon, when he was private secretary, to corral a leader into overworking. One Friday evening, Pierson filled several red boxes with work, leaving a note on the top for the foreign secretary, Ernest Bevin: 'It would be a good idea to do these boxes over the weekend.' On the Monday morning, he returned to find the pile undisturbed but with a postscript added to his note in Bevin's hand: 'Yes, it would.' When he was foreign secretary, Douglas Hurd insisted that programmes for overseas visits include half a day to see something more of a capital city than the inside of its foreign ministry – he liked to visit art galleries and museums (his private secretaries benefited from the diversion, too).

Good leaders take responsibility. When I was in Junior 3, our teacher told us that President Truman had a sign on his desk which read, 'The buck stops here'. Mr Kirrane was eloquent about the meaning of the phrase and what it meant for the president: it was about taking responsibility. No one who was not president could imagine what it was really like to be president and have ultimate responsibility for everything that passed through their in-tray. Every time he looked up from his papers, he read that sign, and every visitor to the Oval Office read it, too. Mr Kirrane seemed not to know that the small sign, presented to Truman by his friend Fred Canfil in the autumn of 1946, was on the president's desk for only a short time. But he was right that its message came to define Truman's presidency. Truman did not shy from taking difficult decisions nor getting involved even when the chances of success were small. He led.

Good leaders have a plan. They have specific ideas for how to change and improve things. No matter the number or complexity of distractions, they can step back and describe what they are striving for overall. They are simplifiers, not complicators. Seneca's advice in the first century BC remains valid: 'No wind is favourable, if you do not know to what port you are heading.' But the vision must be able to encompass the distractions to stay relevant.

Theresa May's statement on the steps on 10 Downing Street on 13 July 2016 was as compelling a manifesto as any prime minister has delivered on their first day in office. Labour friends commiserated with each other: she was going to attempt to do what they would have urged a Labour prime minister to do. Later she had the text of her speech framed and hung outside her office inside the building: it summarised why she was in politics. But it more or less ignored the main item in her in-tray, mentioning 'leaving the European Union' at the end and only in passing. Even new prime ministers cannot dictate the agenda, and her inability to persuade her parliamentary party to endorse her version of leaving the EU prevented her from achieving anything else.

The good leader wears the burden of office lightly. No one is entitled to a leadership position (with the royal family being the last exception in the UK); the whiff of entitlement actively disqualifies candidates these days. But leaders must not be overawed by their responsibilities. A German friend once told me that, before he set off for London on his first visit as a teenager, his father had told him that the great thing about the UK was that serious people did not take themselves seriously – they were able to be the butt of other people's humour without losing face. My friend continued that, over fifty years, he had seen that self-deprecation was the key characteristic of senior Brits; sadly, he added, the same could never be said of senior Germans, rather the reverse. Germans speechify. An important event will begin with half a dozen speeches with all speakers explicitly acknowledging every other important person in the audience. Only once did I witness a chairman declare a premature end to the interminable delivery of introductory remarks by quoting Lord Carrington: 'All the people who matter don't care, and all the people who care don't matter.'

Good leaders convey a sense that they are at ease with their responsibilities. If you do not look as if you are enjoying a job, you will find it difficult to convince people that you are doing it well. I think that that is the essence of charisma: the ability to convey to others the sense that you are doing something important enough not only to interest them but also to make others want to help you. If enthusiasm and energy are not inspiring, in the end they become bombast and self-promotion.

In order to perform well it helps leaders not to think they are doing something superhuman. The presumption on the part of people around them that they can do a difficult job helps them. Of all the people I saw in Downing Street, the one who looked most at home was David Cameron. Vestiges of the idea of the ruling class make Brits feel uncomfortable. The UK has changed, but its history constantly asserts its relevance. The fact is that one school has produced twenty prime ministers in three hundred years (including the first and two of the four most recent). No doubt schoolboy ambitions at Eton are the same as anywhere else, but the role models of 'old boys' make this ambition more plausible. Schoolchildren everywhere aspire to be actors, doctors, and even politicians. The knowledge that Dominic West, John Gurdon, and Boris Johnson all went to your school must make the aspiration feel less fanciful.

Effective leaders tend to be thick-skinned, or at least able to give the plausible impression of being thick-skinned. Prime ministers these days could not function if they read everything written in newspapers or listened to everything said about them on television (not enough hours in the day); most commentary about most leaders in free countries is at the hostile end of questioning. Puff pieces by supporters are just as unhelpful and debilitating. Yet few leaders seem able to follow the Duke of Edinburgh's advice not to read anything at all written about them. The more there is to ignore, the more important it is to ignore it.

Sometimes successful political leaders seem not so much to have a thick skin as to have an incomplete personality. In *Brideshead Revisited*, Julia Flyte observes that her politician husband, Rex Mottram, has something missing: '[He] isn't a real person at all; he's just a few faculties of a man highly developed; the rest simply isn't there.' As a result, he isn't plagued by doubt or self-reflection. Gestures which, coming from others, would look tasteless or obscene (such as presenting her with a tortoise with her initials set in diamonds on its 'living shell') seem stylish and irresistible coming from Rex. His focus and self-confidence are absolute. Political leaders at the peak of their powers share these attributes.

Self-confidence takes a leader a long way, but it needs limits. Lord Melbourne (no shrinking violet himself) once observed of Lord Macaulay: 'I wish I was as cock-sure of anything as Tom Macaulay is of everything.' Melbourne became prime minister; Macaulay became secretary at war and paymaster general, senior political offices but not fulfilling his vaulting ambition. Humility is always part of the successful leadership mix.

Good leaders have a sense of what went before. They

stand on the shoulders of giants whether they are aware of the fact or not, but they do better when they *are* aware. In the UK, public servants know (albeit not enough) about Gladstone, Palmerston, Peel, Wellington, and two Pitts – men who created and moulded the institutions of the modern British state without becoming fabulously wealthy in the process. After victory at Waterloo in 1815, a grateful nation gave the Stratfield Saye estate to the military commander, the Duke of Wellington. His descendant, the ninth duke, still lives there today, each year presenting the monarch with a French standard before 18 June – the anniversary of the battle – to reaffirm the family's occupancy.

No nineteenth-century prime minister retired in penury but none used high office, as first ministers had done in earlier centuries, to become the richest man in the land. Robert Walpole, the first prime minister, was among the last explicitly to exploit the office for personal gain. He built Houghton Hall in Norfolk at a cost (estimated by him) of over £200,000 (equivalent to over £20,000,000 today). In the eighteenth century, everyone accepted that office holders (all unpaid) would use that office to enrich themselves. Corruption was so pervasive that it could be regarded as the system of government rather than a flaw in the system. That diminished in the nineteenth century; by the time the third Marquess of Salisbury stepped down as prime minister in 1902, he felt he must turn down promotion to a dukedom because his family lacked the resources to sustain the highest rank of nobility. Over the nineteenth century, the expectation grew that office holders (still unpaid) were men wealthy and leisured enough to serve their country and community by accepting office. In the twentieth century, government finally recognised that capable people would work for the country only if they were paid: prime ministers and MPs began to be paid in 1911.

Alongside the famous figures of history, commemorated with statues and multiple biographies, are numerous less storied figures, whose legacy is no less remarkable. As secretary of state for war, Robert Haldane reformed the British Army, establishing the Imperial General Staff and the Territorial Army. He co-founded the London School of Economics and Imperial College and prepared the ground for the establishment of MI5, MI6, and the Royal Air Force. In each of these endeavours his role was decisive but not exclusive – the Webbs are better remembered as co-founders of the LSE, and Jan Smuts and Hugh Trenchard had a more prominent role in founding the RAF. But nearly all great endeavours are collaborative.

Prime ministers, like popes and kings, are remembered even when they are not particularly distinguished. Like popes and kings, the eras in which they are in charge carry their name. Some of their cabinet ministers deserve a more widespread reputation. Over the last dozen years, I would single out David Gauke, Dominic Grieve, and David Lidington – competent, hard-working, and principled ministers who always did what they thought was right, despite the pressures (sometimes from above) to do otherwise. One of my favourite scenes in the Harry Potter novels is towards the end of *Harry Potter and the Philosopher's Stone* when, with the whole school assembled in the Great Hall, Dumbledore is tallying final points before awarding the House

Cup. With Gryffindor and Slytherin momentarily tied for the lead, he raises his hand and waits for students to fall silent: 'It takes a great deal of bravery to stand up to our enemies, but just as much to stand up to our friends. I therefore award ten points to Mr Neville Longbottom.' Cue deafening applause from Neville's fellow Gryffindors.

Good leaders are approachable and aware that, for many of those working for them, their seniority means they are not easily approached. Nearly every leader I have seen in action has explicitly claimed at some point to welcome challenge. In Berlin, a leading editor once invited me to attend an editorial meeting. He was personable, funny, and completely clear about what he wanted. Just as clearly, he was used to getting his own way. Towards the end of the meeting, he told his colleagues that his coach had warned him against a tendency to imperiousness; she had encouraged him to seek feedback, particularly from junior colleagues working directly for him. He invited anyone to get in touch; a chat was as welcome as an email. Without knowing anyone else in the room, I would say that their collective expression could be summarised as, 'Yeah, right!'

Good leaders have courage. Philip Larkin said, 'Courage … means not scaring others.' Mrs Thatcher showed that courage on 12 October 1984, when a bomb exploded at 2:54 a.m. in the Grand Hotel, Brighton, where she was staying during the Conservative Party Conference. She was not injured, but five people were killed. Having been led to safety and spending some of the night at a police station, she returned to the conference hall. At 9:30 a.m., when her chief whip, John Wakeham, was still buried in the rubble with his wife dead by his side, when the full extent of the carnage was still not known, she delivered a dignified and defiant speech; her unflappability calmed the country. It also takes courage not to be scared by others. For me, the best party conference speech in my adult life was Neil Kinnock's the following year in Bournemouth, when he took on Militant. Sweating freely, snarling with fury, Kinnock ploughed on, while Eric Heffer walked out and Derek Hatton jeered from the conference floor. Kinnock unflinchingly told his party what was wrong with it.

Maintaining a course that defies the consensus is a test leaders use to measure themselves. Once again, Churchill is the model. In the 1930s, most British politicians quailed before the rise of Nazi Germany. Painfully aware of the vulnerability of the UK, the majority supported Neville Chamberlain's appeasement policy. Because subsequent events proved Churchill right, he is remembered as a hero and Chamberlain as a villain. But the memory of Churchill's achievement is too narrow. As prime minister, Chamberlain understood better than most, including Churchill, the military weakness of the UK – every year he bought in the middle of the decade helped the rearmament effort, which meant that the UK could face the Nazis with greater confidence when conflict began in 1939. The fact that a leader's policy is vindicated does not mean other policies are wholly wrong.

Although those who admired Hitler were a minority, no one had the stomach to oppose him while he rose to power, and few thought he posed a direct threat to the UK once his position was entrenched. But Churchill, vociferously and consistently, spoke of the mortal danger posed by Hitler and the Nazis. Looking back, it is hard for us to understand, still less to forgive, politicians who shrugged their shoulders when Nazi Germany dismembered Czechoslovakia, sponsored a pogrom against the Jews, absorbed Austria, and remilitarised the Rhineland. But the vile nature of Naziism announced itself nearly two years before tanks rolled into the Rhine Valley in 1936.

Who burned down the Reichstag in March 1933 may still be disputed, but details of the Night of the Long Knives on 30 June to 2 July 1934 are not. For thirty-six hours, the Schutzstaffel and Gestapo targeted leaders of the Sturmabteilung in order to dispense with internal opposition to Hitler. At least eighty-five people were killed. At the end of the bloodletting, the Nazi government passed a law legalising everything that had just happened. Democracies needed no more evidence to prove the gravity of the threat posed by the Nazis, and they had every reason from that moment to prepare to fight them. But only Churchill seemed to understand the seriousness and imminence of the threat.

In 2022, the build-up to war in Ukraine uncomfortably echoed the 1930s. Looking back, Putin ordered the poisoning of the Skripals in Salisbury in 2018, intervened in Syria in 2015, annexed Crimea in 2014, invaded Georgia in 2008, and publicly rejected the post-Cold War settlement in 2007. Some commentators (notably Fiona Hill) warned that Putin was hell-bent on reassembling the Russian imperium, but most commentators were flabbergasted when Russian tanks crossed the Ukrainian border on 24 February 2022, heading towards Kyiv. We should pay closer attention to what well-resourced dictators say they will do: when they get the chance, they have the option of trying.

Policymakers missed the seriousness of Putin's ambition. But, since the Second World War, overreaction has been as bad a problem as under-reaction. Churchill's successors have tended to overreact in a bid to emulate his example. In 1956, Anthony Eden considered Gamal Abdel Nasser to pose just as much threat to international order as Hitler when Egypt unilaterally nationalised the Suez Canal Company. He was wrong. In 2003, opposition to fighting alongside the US in Iraq was loud, sustained, and organised. But Tony Blair, blindly supported by Conservatives in the House of Commons, turned a deaf ear to the protests. He felt sure he was right to defy popular opposition to fighting Saddam Hussein. His team fed him the supporting evidence he wanted to read and helped him make the worst foreign policy mistake since Suez. Robin Cook's resignation speech in the Commons on 17 March was not merely magnificent oratory, it was also right in all particulars.

A good leader does not assume the consensus is wrong when they disagree with it. Although almost by definition the consensus cannot be right in all aspects (too sweeping, not nuanced enough), the wisdom of the crowd is worth listening to carefully. Sticking to an analysis or course of action that nobody else supports is more often proof of stubbornness than greatness. The trouble is (with Churchill always in a prime minister's mind) sometimes it is not.

Course corrections are an essential part of good leadership. As my favourite gif reminds us, 'I am wrong' are the hardest words to say in the English language, in the same league as 'I love you' and 'Worcestershire sauce'. Leaders have a bigger and more critical audience when admitting failure. But no one can be a good leader unless they can admit and deal with failure or falling short. The best leaders will need to make few such corrections, but no leader is immune from making some.

Admitting a major policy decision was a mistake is incredibly difficult, especially when you see reason to hope that things will improve. I became Iraq director in the summer of 2006. While I had been in Israel, I had nothing to do with the development of the UK's Iraq policy in the aftermath of the war in 2003. Hundreds of people were working in and on Iraq, spending billions and working tirelessly to improve the lives and prospects of Iraqis. Within a few weeks of taking over, I visited Basra and Baghdad. It was impossible to conclude, three and a half years after the war, that the situation on the ground was good or had a realistic prospect of improving. When I returned home, I wrote a long minute, proposing that we begin to wind down our commitment, because no amount of new resource could alter the fact that we had lost. A copy went into the prime minister's box and was returned covered in his red ink scrawl. He disagreed with my analysis and prescription. Copies of my minute went to other private offices around Whitehall. I believe (because it makes sense rather than because I have evidence) that the fact that Gordon Brown agreed with me was the main reason he asked me to be his foreign policy adviser when he became prime minister the following year. When I asked him later, he had forgotten.

Jack Straw used to say that the key attribute of a good

leader was the ability to take decisions. I was surprised the first time I heard this: it seemed so obvious. 'Just you watch!' he advised. So I did. And I observed that many ministers and senior officials find it difficult to reach a decision that will carry their name. Years later, a permanent secretary colleague told me of a secretary of state (generally a pleasure to work with) who always asked for more research or more time and who would, after a decision had definitively been taken, still phone late at night in the hope of delaying a press release prepped for the following morning. Nearly always, leaders must take decisions in the absence of complete facts; they must use their judgement and experience to complement the known facts. If they are good, that will be enough.

People change their minds. As Keynes implied, it is the sensible thing to do when facts change. A leader changing their mind is not a problem per se. It is a problem when a leader pretends they have not changed their mind when they have, or fails to acknowledge the impact on others of the change of mind (including wasted work), or tries to reopen a decision that everyone else thinks has already been taken. Reacting badly when colleagues have failed to anticipate a change of mind is even worse. Good leaders are not capricious.

Prime ministers are the most exposed and lonely decision makers in the UK. As his foreign policy adviser, I had to take part in an exercise with Gordon Brown that imagined a passenger airliner had deviated from its flight plan, was failing to respond to air traffic control, and was heading towards central London. The exercise was brief; the whole point was to recreate the drama of the real-life situation it imagined. Gordon had to decide whether to scramble the RAF (easy: yes) and all-too-quickly he had to decide whether to shoot over two hundred civilians out of the sky in order, possibly, to save thousands of lives on the ground (very, very hard). At the last minute, in the exercise, the pilot of the airliner responded to the visual signals of the pilot of one of the fighter aircraft sent to investigate, and he switched to an emergency channel after discovering his main comms had failed.

The plane landed safely. But, even though it was an exercise, it was a harrowing experience for the PM. The time from first alert to final decision was less than half an hour. He had only a couple of people on the line to advise him and no one in the room with him. He wailed about inadequate facts but recognised that that was the point. And then he had to nominate two cabinet colleagues to take his place in a real-life situation, if he could not be reached in the minutes available. Some decisions, though hard, have to be taken. Leaders take them. Good leaders take the decision that, more often than not, proves to be right.

No matter how talented (and how lucky) a leader is, they will make mistakes; some decisions will subsequently be seen to be wrong. Good leaders know that they make mistakes and do not pretend otherwise. They do not blame other people for their mistakes; they correct them quickly and then learn from them. In other words, they do not make the same mistake twice. But they do not obsess over their mistakes. They know that, although mistakes are unavoidable, they are not inherently a good thing. So, they try to avoid making mistakes and make relatively few.

Good leaders are not deflected by setbacks – as Jack Straw used to say, they 'stick to the knitting'. Ignoring the noise of critics, they get on with the job and the agenda they set out before their election. Leaders have the option of picking their battles and occasionally pulling their punches. Of course, sometimes the setback will objectively be too big to be brazened out. When Theresa May suffered the worst defeat in the House of Commons in 700 years, she soldiered on but politically she was a dead woman walking. But most crises can be defused with a clear political head. As Macmillan observed, 'Quiet, calm deliberation disentangles every knot.'

Dealing honestly and openly with mistakes and failures is a key attribute of a good leader. Occasionally, a leader will be able to turn a defeat into the beginnings of a victory. Maximising the positive is fair enough, as long as 'maximising' does not mean ignoring key facts. On 4 June 1940, Churchill addressed the House of Commons for thirty-five minutes. He admitted that one week earlier, nearly the whole British Army had seemed on the point of being captured. Yet 'a miracle of deliverance' had been accomplished. The RAF had shot down four German planes for every British plane lost, enabling the Royal Navy, and a thousand smaller volunteer vessels, to evacuate over ten times the number of men originally thought possible. The last French troops were lifted from beaches in the Pas-de-Calais earlier that day.

Churchill cautioned that the British 'must be very careful not to assign to this deliverance the attributes of a victory. Wars are not won by evacuations.' He also noted that, while the men were saved, their equipment was not – almost all the army's kit was abandoned in France. Britain should be thankful for the army's return, yet also understand the country had suffered a 'colossal military disaster'.

The evacuation from Dunkirk is as important for Britain's view of itself as the defeat of the Armada in 1588. The rescue of over 340,000 soldiers (including over 100,000 French) gave the UK the minimum force needed to defend itself over the next four years and provided the core of the UK's contribution to Allied forces in the D-Day landings. It allowed England to continue to boast that the country had successfully resisted foreign invasion since 1066 (because Parliament invited William of Orange to land, his invasion in 1688 is never counted as a 'home defeat'). Churchill's response is the template for his successors dealing with bad news. But the key characteristic of this response was not proclaiming that defeat was in fact victory – it was admitting soberly the full extent of the disaster before suggesting a way through. Some of his successors, including those who most closely aspire to model themselves on his example, seem to forget the need for comprehensive and speedy honesty when dealing with bad news.

People like certainty, and they prefer good news to bad; leaders like to please the people they lead. Leaders may be tempted to talk with greater certainty and greater positivity than they know is justified by the facts. A relieved audience applauds more warmly, but eventually over-claiming will be exposed and the audience will remember the earlier deception.

Dealing with setbacks is hard, but it is hardest when the

leader personally carries responsibility for the setback. A positive record and high reputation can be erased by one whopping failure. Tony Blair will always carry responsibility for the UK's involvement in the Second Iraq War; David Cameron for holding a referendum on the UK's continued membership of the EU; and Boris Johnson for negotiating the hardest possible Brexit.

My history teacher did not think any event could be considered 'history' until all protagonists were dead. Until then, you were studying 'current affairs'. But, at twenty years' distance, as the Second Iraq War edges towards the history books, it looks increasingly like a mistake. Participation damaged the reputation of all its external participants. Apart from Blair personally, I know almost no one who supported the Iraq War at the time (who is not Israeli) who still thinks UK involvement a good idea. The idea that Blair had been acting to uphold the rules of the international system dissolved when unfettered inspectors failed to find evidence of WMD anywhere inside Iraq.

Reassessing controversial policies as you proceed is best. To double down is the choice that requires least thought, which may be one reason it is so appealing as a policy choice. As Iraq deteriorated after the fall of Saddam Hussein, Blair devoted more of his energy, and more British blood and treasure, to rectifying the situation. Success was so important to his legacy that fundamental recalibration was impossible while he remained in office. His requirement was so clear that the British system did not feel able to challenge him to his face, no matter the hesitations in private. Gordon Brown had to replace Blair before the

British system could present new options to the prime minister and begin to implement what had been unthinkable to Blair – a phased withdrawal.

Six years after the referendum the jury is still considering its verdict about Brexit. As Zhou Enlai might have said: 'It's too soon to tell.' Half the country still thinks Brexit a good idea; the 48% who voted in favour of EU membership similarly seems not to have changed their mind. Boris Johnson's challenge was that he led one side in the campaign but then had to lead the whole country. The day of the result, Philip Hammond told me that EU-supporting members of the Conservative Party, particularly the parliamentary party, would reconcile themselves quickly to the idea of leaving the EU; he was right. By and large, they accepted the result more quickly than EU-supporters in the wider community. This fact might explain why this government has paid scant attention (most strikingly in Scotland and Northern Ireland, where the majority wanted to remain in the EU) to the concerns of voters who wanted to stay. Behaving as if the 'winner takes all' has done nothing to reconcile the 48% to the fate they rejected.

The case for Brexit continues to be made in terms that appeal only to those who voted for it. The government has not explained what 'taking back control' means in a globalised world. Sovereignty is not what it used to be – certainly not when Palmerston dictated to foreigners, nor even when Eden was defying his main ally (and common sense) in 1956. The ability to negotiate and sign the UK's own trade deals is the benefit most widely trumpeted. Yet whenever a new deal is reported to the House of Lords, the minister at the despatch box fails to answer David Hannay's unvarying question: 'In what way is the new agreement superior from the UK point of view to the one it replaces?' Remainers are invited to accept the new status quo, as decided by a government that feels no need to accommodate or persuade them. Churchill said that one of the principles underpinning his memoir of the Second World War was: 'In victory, magnanimity.' Good leaders are generous to those they defeat.

History remembers almost no one, which is why those who want to be remembered give it a helping hand by writing copious memoirs. In the 1,000-page abridged version of his 6-volume series *The Second World War*, Churchill mentioned Stalingrad on just three pages. Where other commentators identified a wider series of turning points, he fixed in the minds of British readers the idea that the spring of 1940 counted for most. Robert Rhodes James tried to reappraise Churchill's place in British history, but *A Study in Failure* was swamped by Randolph Churchill and Martin Gilbert's eight-volume biography. Nobody disputes Churchill's importance in defeating Nazi Germany; the most likely alternative prime minister (Halifax) would probably have sued for peace in the summer of 1940. Yet the idea that ultimate success excuses earlier failures (even disasters) is questionable, and the idea that those failures contributed to ultimate success or were even indispensable to that success (because they shaped his subsequent leadership) is highly questionable.

Even people whose memory is celebrated by the erection of a statue shortly after their death are largely forgotten a century later. In London, Trafalgar Square is prime real estate for public statuary. Five full-size statues are dotted around Lutyens's fountains: two kings (Charles I and George IV), one admiral, and two generals. Kings whose descendants keep the family throne are widely memorialised. And Horatio Nelson is the UK's greatest naval hero. But not one Briton in ten thousand now knows the exploits of Sir Henry Havelock, who recaptured Cawnpore from sepoy rebels in 1857, or Sir Charles Napier, who telegraphed his conquest – defying explicit orders – of Sindh in 1843 with a single word, 'Peccavi' ('I have sinned').

Sometimes, the commemorated do not need to wait even a century for their legacy to evaporate. In the 1990s, my opposite number at the American Embassy in Riyadh, who had previously served in Conakry, drew my attention to the example of Ahmed Sékou Touré in our discussions about the likely longevity of the House of Saud. As the UK and France left Africa in the 1950s, successor regimes constructed new forms of government, usually self-consciously contrasted with the colonial power's, which they hoped would be an enduring replacement to administration by Europeans. The Gold Coast was first to wrest independence from the UK, becoming Ghana in 1957. Under Kwame Nkrumah, Ghana's government was socialist, nationalist, and non-aligned (which meant it listened more to Moscow and Beijing than London, Paris, and Washington). Two years after amending the constitution in 1964 to make Ghana a one-party state, the police and army (backed by the CIA) deposed the president-for-life. He fled to Guinea, where President Touré ruled according to a system he called Nkrumah-Touréism. Touré's admiration for his deposed near-neighbour was strong enough for him to invite Nkrumah to be co-president, which he remained until his death in 1972.

Ten years later, Ahmed Sékou Touré was elected to a fourth seven-year term as president of Guinea. His hold over his country appeared absolute, his political philosophy entrenched in the constitution. Yet, without him, the hold of Nkrumah-Touréism proved tenuous. On 25 March 1984, while visiting Saudi Arabia, Touré suffered a heart attack. His hosts arranged an immediate medevac to the United States, but he died at the Cleveland Clinic the next day. On 3 April, the military seized power, deposing the acting president and dissolving Touré's Democratic Party of Guinea. A system of government intended to be an enduring model for the whole of Africa collapsed less than one week after the death of its founder.

Leaders cannot control posterity and are likely to be revealed as foolish if they try, even if they aren't around to witness full proof of their foolishness. Good leaders plan for the future but know they cannot dictate the future. They focus on the here and now, knowing that success now is more likely to endure after they've gone.

My first attempt at the opening sentence of this paragraph ran: 'If Touré ever read Shelley, he failed to understand *Ozymandias*; thirty years after his death, his legacy does not amount to even "two vast and trunkless legs".' I rewrote it when I realised I was contradicting one of my main motives in writing this book. Leadership is hard. Most people assessing a leader's performance are generally unsympathetic; some will be implacably hostile. Touré was the first president of a country inadequately prepared by the colonial power for independence. At the founding of the Fifth Republic in 1958, de Gaulle gave French colonies a stark choice: more autonomy but with ultimate power remaining in Paris, or independence. Guineans voted overwhelmingly for independence. In the campaign 'independence' meant 'getting rid of France'; what that meant in practice was not addressed. The institutions of the state, such as they were, had been staffed by expatriate French (who quickly disappeared) and a few Guineans trained in Paris. In effect, the new state was an ill-equipped laboratory, where Touré experimented with ideas learned on a US campus. The country boasted impressive natural resources: gold (the country gave its name to Britain's gold coins in the eighteenth century) and one quarter of the world's proven bauxite reserves. And yet the main beneficiaries of those resources continued to be foreigners. Civil servants in the new government struggled in an unequal negotiation with international business people and lawyers who still adjudicated the rules. No matter his manifest shortcomings, Touré was set up to fail.

Unlike African presidents-for-life, British prime ministers often look better in the rear-view mirror: the reputation of John Major, Gordon Brown, and Theresa May has waxed in retirement. Having invariably entered office with their best approval ratings, regard for PMs seems to reach its nadir the day they retire: 'All political careers end in failure.' Churchill, offered a dukedom (declined) and the Garter (accepted) in the weeks before his planned retirement, summarised his feelings by misquoting Milton:

So much I feel my genial spirits droop,
My hopes all flat.
Nature within me seems in all her purposes weary of
herself.

Melancholy at the finish is part of the deal. And yet candidates for leadership do not dwell on the downside: they line up in an apparently inexhaustible supply for the top political jobs. Many candidates appear dazzled by the perks. Colin Powell was contemptuous of what he called 'limo fever', the obsession with the trappings of high office. Being there, rather than doing something worthwhile whilst there, often appears to be a major motivation. But simply reaching the top does not make you a leader.

Superficial candidates are not exposed in the modern selection process. There is a fashionable view that the more people involved in making any choice, the more democratic (and therefore better) it must be. It is true that the old system, when leaders emerged from the parliamentary party, was fatally and deservedly discredited after Macmillan anointed Douglas-Home in 1963. For a time, parliamentary parties then elected one of their own. These days, however, in the Conservative and Labour parties, MPs merely winnow down leadership candidates for a vote of the entire party membership.

The late twentieth-century system of parliamentary parties selecting party leaders was better; it gave short shrift to candidates whose main qualification was the adoration of the party conference. Your parliamentary colleagues see you in all conditions, not just the controlled conditions of a TV debate or scripted conference speech; they are less easily impressed. The parliamentary Labour Party would never have chosen Jeremy Corbyn as leader; at the outset of the leadership competition, he did not have sufficient parliamentary support to proceed to the next stage; old stagers had to lend him their vote for him to be nominated at all.

The role of prime minister is grindingly hard work. Yet the number of candidates indicates that many who aspire to the job have not reflected deeply about its content. It is almost impossible to do well. You have to convincingly represent the country on the international stage from day one. You have to take life and death decisions based on information you cannot fully share and on less information than you would like. You have to make tough choices that materially disadvantage some of the people you are leading; shirking or delaying a decision will often have the impact of a conscious decision, and you will be responsible for the negative consequences of what you fail to do as well as of what you do. You will juggle twenty different subject matters in any given day. You will need plausibly to act as if you are the best informed participant in any meeting if you are to persuade other participants that you deserve to sit in the chair. You will achieve that only by unrelenting hard work.

No matter how secure a prime minister appears in office, alternatives are always on the mind of parliamentarians, if only because a debilitating accident or heart attack are ever-present possibilities for the middle-aged. At any given moment, most candidates who dream of replacing the prime minister do not have the basic qualities for this

most demanding job. For jobs in public life, the importance of aptitude and experience is less obvious than, say,
for fighter pilots or brain surgeons, but it is just as real. In
the RAF and NHS, most aspirants are weeded out because
their unsuitability is spotted long before they are allowed
to settle behind the controls of a Typhoon jet or to wield
a scalpel. Political training is just as important; it prepares
the best and reveals the shortcomings of the rest.

Until Margaret Thatcher became prime minister in 1979,
long experience in multiple ministerial roles was the norm
for someone taking on the top job. She broke the mould
and, for half the electorate, was wildly successful. Tony
Blair and David Cameron became PM with not one day
of previous ministerial experience between them, and shattered the remaining fragments, but perhaps the mould is
worth gluing back together.

Encouraged, I suspect, by the opening paragraphs of the
CVs of recent prime ministers, most people I have met in
British politics have imagined themselves in the top job. I
cannot claim that any has asked for my advice, but here it is
for anyone who wants to lead at any level: if you want to be
a good leader, you need intelligence, judgement, discipline,
and 'bottom', all demonstrated over time, doing work relevant to the leadership position you aspire to.

The proof of 'intelligence' is emphatically not the passing
of public examinations. It seems significant to me that no
one since I started work ever asked me about the class of
my degree (a 2:1). In the workplace bosses value different
proofs of intelligence: they are more interested in speed and
accuracy of work, in concision, in fluency, in the ability to

incorporate everything that needs to be addressed in the depth it needs to be addressed, in the ability to winnow out irrelevant information, in the ability to process new material and to move when facts change.

Good judgement is acquired over time. Teenagers' judgement is not their defining characteristic. Countries and organisations depend on the judgement of their leaders for success. At the top, the quality of a person's judgement is exposed like nowhere else. So much more is required than in the jobs along the way, so that those choosing top leaders can never be sure if a candidate has what it takes. But a track record is an indication. Along the way, has the person made the right calls, secured the best outcomes, mitigated the worst ones, fought battles it was important to win (and won them) and avoided unnecessary battles, appointed capable people, correctly assessed problems and placed their effort most effectively in solving those problems, been able to prioritise and to delegate, been able to give a compelling account for choices that did not subsequently work out as hoped?

Discipline is as essential as it is mundane. Can you manage your time? Can you tackle tasks in the order they need to be accomplished (rather than the order that appeals most to you)? Can you knuckle down and do the elements of a job that do not appeal to you but that are vital to doing it well? Can you set the example a team requires for a leader in a given job – of integrity, industry, and altruism?

Thirty years ago, the Number 1 Board of the Foreign Office, in some of its most heated discussions, would use the idea of 'bottom' as a tiebreaker. The tied candidates for a top ambassadorship would have equally impressive CVs, equally relevant experience, and equal fluency in the relevant language; they would boast good judgement and admirable discipline. But which one would you want in the job in the middle of an unforeseen crisis? Who could the Board imagine getting a foreign government to do something it did not particularly want to do but that was vital for the UK? Who would rally the troops when they were sitting in the basement awaiting evacuation? Who would help the team get through in one piece? In short, who was the more solid?

Solidity sounds unexciting, but fizz and style wear thin in crisis. 'Sûrtout, pas trop de zèle,'* Talleyrand is alleged to have said, coining diplomats' single favourite piece of advice. Every diplomat I have ever respected has trotted out the quotation at some point. Although when forensically examined they all meant to stress something slightly different, the centre of the Venn diagram is consistent: when times are tough or uncertain, there is a premium on calm, moderation, method, tenacity, and stamina, on colleagues who act in the knowledge that one day they will be held to account.

Four key attributes are already at least one too many to be a memorable list. But good leaders need to be even more: they need to be clear, consistent, curious, collaborative, courageous, and compassionate. These are characteristics general to all people rather than particular to leaders; not everyone can possess intelligence, good judgement,

---

* 'Above all, not too much zeal.'

discipline, and 'bottom', but everyone should have the six 'c's. Leaders with these characteristics are good to be around, make the world a better place, and make others want to make the world a better place. They motivate people. Gordon Brown could be as difficult a boss as any I have had, but once or twice he displayed a compassion and vulnerability that overrode a hundred difficult moments. Early on 25 February 2009, news broke that David and Samantha Cameron's six-year-old son, Ivan, had died in the night. Gordon immediately asked the Speaker to suspend business in the House of Commons for the day. For a moment, the prime minister and the leader of the opposition were united in grief; more than any couple in politics, Gordon and Sarah, who lost their first child, Jennifer, when she was ten days old, knew what the Camerons were suffering and wanted to help.

If you want to lead, you have to be prepared to be lonely – not all the time but some of the time, and at most crucial times. Some of the biggest decisions are explicitly and exclusively for the boss. At those moments, you need people around you who will tell you everything you need to know, people who feel able to speak up when they think you are heading in the wrong direction, who want to protect you, who are willing to work as hard as you do, who become an extension of your capacity and who, because of all of that, increase your chances of coming through safely to the other side.

Sue Nye was chief of staff to Neil Kinnock when he was leader of the Labour Party and Gordon Brown when he was shadow chancellor; she was Gordon's political secretary in Number 10. Reflecting on what the two leaders had in common, she said that fundamentally they were optimists; no matter how dire a situation appeared to others, they firmly believed that 'something would turn up'. Sometimes they were wrong but sometimes they were right, and that is what kept them going.

Even good leaders are mostly forgotten. Last year, I exchanged warm messages with Julian Gillmore about my old boss, David. He was glad to be reminded of what his father had done, by someone outside of his family, twenty years after his death. A leader's impact is often too local, too limited in time, and too little trumpeted to linger in the memory of strangers. But fame is not their motive: it is enough to do their best, to do the right thing, to leave things better than they found them. They earn Mary Ann Evans's epitaph for Dorothea Brooke in *Middlemarch*:

> Her full nature, like that river of which Cyrus broke the strength, spent itself in channels which had no great name on earth. But the effect of her being on those around her was incalculably diffusive: for the growing good of the world is partly dependent on unhistoric acts; and that things are not so ill with you and me as they might have been, is half owing to the number who lived faithfully a hidden life, and rest in unvisited tombs.

10

Self-Assessment

I've never read a self-assessment that was less than shining, humblebrags only adding to the gloss ('My main fault is that I drive myself too hard'). In theory, we know we are not perfect, but in practice we fear to share that knowledge with our line managers. My self-assessment as PUS is no different.

My predecessor announced his intention to step down during the general election campaign of 2015. I read the long prospectus and submitted my application just after the competition went live, immediately after David Cameron returned to Downing Street. After a sift and two interviews, Jeremy Heywood phoned at the end of July to tell me I had got the job. The main focus of the application process was on how I would go about implementing a 25% cut in the FCO's operating budget. I wanted the job, so I engaged with the premise but felt that concessions conceded in an interview were not written in bureaucratic blood. I went on holiday as planned, went to the Schützenfest (county fair) in Neuss at the end of August, and started on 1 September. I had forty-eight hours between jobs.

One of the first pieces of paper to cross my desk was a welcome message for me to send everyone in the Office. In the whirl, I had not prepared anything, so it was good to have a draft. But the draft was a shock: an apparently unobjectionable boilerplate that anyone might have said and no one in their right mind would want others to mistake for their innermost thoughts. I took a blank sheet of paper and wrote my own message.

Starting the last job in my Diplomatic Service career, I thought first of the beginning. I thought about Salford, and told colleagues about where I was from. Seven years later, where I am from seems even more important when explaining what I was trying to do.

As a child, my world was tiny. I was born in Hope Hospital, which served the towns immediately to the west of Manchester. Until I was eighteen, I never lived further than a thirty-minute walk from that hospital; my primary school was two miles away, and my grammar school half a mile away. Most of my family and all my friends lived in Salford. I imagined the city had always looked the same as when I was a child: sooty, solid, but gradually decaying. In the early 1970s edition of the *Guinness Book of Records* we had at home, Salford featured once: as the place in Europe with the highest death rate.

When I visited the National Archives as PUS, I was welcomed with a small display of historic documents about my hometown. Until the second half of the eighteenth century, it had been wholly rural; most of the land was owned by the Earl of Derby. Among the farms were a few large houses: Robert Clive used to spend childhood holidays with relations at Hope Hall (now demolished); Ordsall Hall (prettiest), and Wardley Hall (residence of bishops of

Salford) still stand, but Agecroft Hall was sold to an American tobacco millionaire who shipped it piece by piece to Virginia in the 1920s.

Salford was always, in a small way, a centre for weaving, but Robert Arkwright's invention of the spinning frame in the 1760s transformed the place from producing yards of fustian in cottages to miles of cotton in the biggest factories in the world. The Duke of Bridgewater opened one of England's earliest canals in 1761 to get the product to market. The town's population ballooned from 12,000 in 1812 to 220,000 by the end of the nineteenth century. The new population was housed in rows of back-to-back, two-up, two-down, brick-built terraces, with up to eighty dwellings per acre. Living conditions were miserable and provided Friedrich Engels with source material for *The Condition of the Working Class in England* (1845). Engels was the eldest son of a wealthy German industrialist who owned cotton mills in Wuppertal and Salford; in his twenties, he was reluctantly dispatched to run the family's Salford businesses. Local legend claimed he tried to found the first Communist Party in The Grapes pub in Eccles, but even stinking squalor failed to rile the town's workers.

The only story my mother's father told me about his father concerned the hustings before the 1929 general election. Our family home was in the Salford West constituency, created in 1885 and held by Liberal and Conservative MPs until the massive expansion of the franchise in the 1920s. My grandfather, who had just turned thirteen, was excited to attend his first rally and proud when his father asked the Conservative MP a question: what was his position regarding the local Catholic population, now that the British government had recognised the Irish Free State? Mr Astbury replied that the Irish should go home, and my great grandfather led a Catholic exodus from the hall. Astbury lost the seat to the Labour candidate.

The town peaked at the beginning of the twentieth century. In nine months in 1905 in Pendlebury, Acme built a massive mill that employed 500 workers who kept 117,000 spindles spinning yarn. It was a prolonged last gasp (coinciding with the granting of city status in 1926); the mill operated for just fifty years before cheaper production overseas choked it and most local industry. Lowry painted the mill in its heyday for a local doctor who gave the canvas to his son as a reminder of home when he went to Oxford. The empty Acme carcass loomed silently over the playground of my primary school. Grime, silence, and water-logged bomb sites were the backdrop to my childhood.

The backdrop contrasted starkly with the foreground, and it was so depressing that I focused all my attention on the latter, the community, the people who kept things going. The church and school were key: close-knit, mutually supportive, patriotic, proud, and demanding. Monsignor Egan at St Mary's set the standard for scholarship and altruism. His name was printed at the bottom of service booklets in all churches in the diocese; he was vicar general and imprimatur of the new-fangled English version of the Mass. His visits to our primary school were accompanied by a buzz as palpable as for a royal. The desire of the headmaster and his staff to impress him conveyed itself to their pupils, equally keen to please the smiling old man in black.

At secondary school, K. C. Conroy explained that decay had not been my hometown's permanent state. The tomato-soup-coloured water of the Bridgewater Canal had once been the sparkling artery connecting Salford to the outside world. Joule House on the Crescent opposite the main campus of Salford University was the birthplace and first laboratory of the physicist who gave his name to the building and to the unit of energy; Joule was not a fancy Frenchman but a Salfordian. The Pankhursts, Britain's first suffragettes, lived in Seedley Park, a stone's throw from our classroom. KC planted the idea that decay was not the city's inevitable fate.

From my bedroom, I could see the Pennines: good things were on the horizon. Or over the horizon. I left at the first opportunity and never lived there again. But, more or less coinciding with my departure, Salford's economic fortunes began to improve. The litter-clogged canals were cleared. Industrial architecture became fashionable and was restored. The last estates of terraced houses in Ordsall and Chimney Pot Park were spared the wrecking ball and refurbished instead. Manchester United, whose stadium – despite their name – was in Salford, became the most famous and most profitable football club in the world. Lowry's paintings became internationally collectible (*The Mill, Pendlebury* sold for £2.6 million in 2020). And the BBC transferred half its English operations to Salford's Media City.

I am one of those northerners who, as Brian Redhead used to complain, extols the virtues of the north from the comfort of the south of England. My life moved in a different direction, but it started, indelibly, in Salford. Every ambition started there. My mum first got me thinking by quoting (perhaps, misquoting) Voltaire: 'I want to be an ancestor.' As a callow youth, that seemed like a worthy starting point.

Everything I value, I learned to value in Salford. At De La Salle, the brothers taught us to think. They were so comfortable in their Catholic faith that they assumed their arguments would confirm us in the religion of our baptism. They were half right. After university scraped away religion, the example of people who had in effect taught me ethics remained: honest, caring, and exacting. Discarding God, I embraced their standard of what counted as a good life, making the most of your talents, helping others, harming no one, making the world a better place in whatever way you could.

I learned that nothing in history is fixed, and no event and no person is subject to only one uncontested interpretation. I learned that everything, no matter how apparently hopeless, can be improved if many people join together. I learned that the world needs to be a better place and only people, generally those on the ground closest to the problem, can do that; nothing good happens of its own accord. The Foreign Office was the place I made my contribution.

Looking back, the most unnecessary thing I did in the Foreign Office was strive to fit in. I arrived in a neo-classical building full of men wearing suits, white or blue shirts, silk ties, and shiny, black Oxford shoes. Forty years later my uniform of dark suit and Church's shoes feels authentically mine, but so do chinos and crocs. I was institutionalised before the institution decided to relax some old expectations. These days you can wear whatever makes you feel most comfortable, compatible with not shocking the foreigners you work with.

Looking forward, the best piece of management advice I would most like to pass on is this: if someone does something wrong, let them know quickly and in private; tell them exactly what was wrong, and how they might have done better, and move on. If they repeat the mistake, have a second, clearer conversation (the first attempt at a difficult conversation is often less clear than the initiator hopes).

Whenever a professional relationship went agley, it was usually because I had failed to follow that advice. The most important childhood lesson, learnt from family, teachers, and priests, was that you should treat everyone, always, with the same kindness and respect you expect from them. What is true in general is even truer for leaders. A team takes its cue from its leader. Team members tend to learn most from their leader. If their leader is impatient or rude or directive, then they will excuse such behaviour in themselves. The health and productivity of any organisation rests on its leaders embodying the principles the organisation claims to value most. When leaders do not, their bosses have to step up and step in.

I remember in particular, and uncomfortably, how I handled others' unhappiness with two senior colleagues. My personal relationship with each could not have been more different: I had known one for many years ('X'), the other only since the day my appointment as PUS was announced ('Y'). But, on reflection, the characters, strengths, and weaknesses of X and Y were similar: stylish, energetic, warm, a bit iconoclastic, and a bit Marmite, adored by some, avoided by others.

Both were on the cusp of big new jobs when complaints were made. Both were ferociously ambitious and adept at gruntling ministers. Part of their talent lay in knowing how to talk to politicians (combining respect with knowing how to disagree) and part of their talent lay in delivering what ministers wanted. Although the two would describe their methods differently, both approaches boiled down to setting high standards and driving their teams hard: 'You can't make an omelette without breaking eggs'. They were both resistant to (or more accurately, preternaturally sensitive to) receiving feedback; development conversations were defensive or awkward, and then rare. Both were breaking new ground and had found progress through the senior management structure difficult; both felt their managers should make explicit allowance for that difficulty.

The way complaints were logged was relevant. For X, it was an unsigned letter delivered to my office; later (no doubt after the complainant had found my handling inadequate) an identical anonymous letter arrived at the cabinet secretary's office. For Y, it was a formal complaint, logged by a number of named colleagues.

The anonymity of the complaint against X determined my reaction: a conversation rather than an investigation. It was awkward, with me conceding that the whistle-blower had given no evidence as well as no name; I had to admit that the basis for urging a recalibration of behaviour was flimsy.

For Y, I instituted a full investigation, as thorough as any in my time, led by a senior colleague. I made a mistake early on by agreeing that, because the colleague was on loan from the Home Civil Service, the cabinet secretary should be the ultimate arbiter rather than me. The report was comprehensive and damning: the complaints were upheld; the investigator concluded that, had the colleague been a member of the Diplomatic Service, the colleague's promotion, then imminent, would have been paused or cancelled.

Jeremy Heywood excluded me from the final stages of the investigation, in which he decided, because of an apparent discrepancy between the formal report and the accompanying signed witness statements, that the report's conclusions were unsound. I was aware that witnesses had spoken freely to the investigator because they felt that they were in a 'safe space'; they were more circumspect in what they signed because those statements, they knew, would be shared with the target of the investigation, who – if the promotion were confirmed – would remain in a position of professional power over them. The investigator later assured me that, despite the apparent discrepancy between the report and supporting statements, he would not have changed any of his report: it accurately reflected what he had discovered.

The rejection of the report was treated as the exoneration of the colleague. Various developmental suggestions were made; none was followed up. The promotion stood. And a large swathe of the Office was confirmed in the already widely held view that complaining was more likely to damage the complainant professionally than the target of the complaint.

I can count my subsequent tête-à-tête conversations with Y on my thumbs, both occasions when I might have helped with Y's further Civil Service ambitions. X, on the other hand, remains a friend. Neither learned anything positive from their episode; both would be stronger officers if they had. At the least, I was complicit in their failure to learn.

X and Y were good officers. I would judge that X was exceptional, while Y was several steps behind. My judgement of their professional excellence and the importance of the contribution they were already making and could potentially make in future affected my actions; it also affected the cabinet secretary's actions. When problems are close to home, objectivity is tested to breaking point and sometimes breaks. My conclusion is that complaints procedures against colleagues in higher grades have to be taken out of the hands of other senior civil servants. Until investigations and imposition of sanctions are independent of the senior Civil Service, junior civil servants will never have confidence in them. And they are right not to have confidence.

The second best piece of advice was: always ask yourself who will be most upset at any decision, and to what extent will their upset be justified? The author of this advice was the non-executive member of the Senior Appointments Board (SAB), who took me aside after I explained at an early meeting of the SAB my ambition to achieve better gender balance in senior appointments. The SAB continued to appoint the best candidate but unapologetically became more active in broadening the field of candidates for all jobs, and in helping candidates from under-represented groups to prepare better. Strong male officers have nothing to fear from under-represented groups being given a fair crack of the whip.

And the third often-remembered piece of advice was Patrick Mayhew's, via Jack Straw: 'Dear boy, whenever you find yourself in the detritus, and you will, just put your paws up.' Quickly. I tried – examples are seared in my memory, the details of which would embarrass me to repeat. But sometimes, as a leader, you have to put your paws up for a mistake that you do not think was yours or that you feel less grave than others do. I had to give evidence before the Foreign Affairs Select Committee (FASC) shortly after the coronavirus pandemic engulfed the world, just after the UK had left the EU. Countries were still deciding the extent to which they wanted to work together on different parts of Covid-19 policy. Early on, the EU invited the UK to join its programme to develop a vaccine. Kate Bingham, who led the UK vaccine programme, has described the conditions attached to the EU's offer: Brussels would lead; the UK would hand over all its work to date; and Brussels would decide the order in which participating countries received any vaccine resulting from the programme. She found those conditions too onerous. The government accepted her recommendation not to participate.

For some reason, at an even earlier stage in consultations (that is, in February, the month after Brexit) the government decided to dwell on the fact that officials in Brussels had initially tried to make contact with British colleagues using redundant email addresses. Ministers implied that these emails were the only way EU officials had tried to get in touch. The line was that EU incompetence had precluded UK participation in an EU vaccination programme. Which was not true. British officials in Brussels had taken part in several meetings in which the programme was discussed, meetings that were reported to the Department of Health in London.

While giving evidence to the FASC in March 2020, I was asked if ministers had been briefed about what was happening in Brussels and replied, 'Yes.' I was wrong. I did not know whether or not DoH officials had briefed ministers (I discovered later that they had not). I also agreed with a committee member's suggestion that the decision not to take part was political. Immediately after my evidence session, one of Dominic Raab's special advisers phoned to complain that I had not followed the narrative (that the EU had cocked up). In the same conversation I realised that I had made a mistake by claiming that ministers (rather than officials) had been informed of the EU offer, so I decided to sign a letter of apology drafted by SpAds.

I had screwed up; my contrition would be believed if I said sorry in words chosen by those I had offended. But I was puzzled by the lack of confidence in Brexit. We had left the EU, so it struck me as logical that the UK would choose to go its own way in developing a vaccine rather than deal with the likely bureaucracy involved in joining an EU programme. Moreover, the decision was the first opportunity to demonstrate the advantages of independence from Brussels. Within six months, Kate Bingham and the scientists she worked with had justified the decision for the UK to go its own way.

Leading an old institution, you know you are merely a custodian; the fundamentals were fixed long before you turned up and will still be evident long after you depart. You can change emphasis but the only overhaul that works is one that reconnects with core principles. Di Lampedusa got it right in *The Leopard*: sometimes everything must change if everything is to stay the same. As an organisation, the Foreign Office stresses excellence: to be the best diplomats, to command the attention of key international meetings grappling with the most complicated and most important problems of the day, it needs the best people. That essential requirement does not change.

But what constitutes the 'best people' is utterly different from when the Office reformed itself after the First World War and again after the Second World War. Excellence was once white, male, wealthy, and aristocratic, because rich, white, male aristocrats decided what was considered excellent and restricted (importantly, never completely denied) access to the resources (particularly education) that would have helped others meet their standard. Excellence is now more democratic; no group has failed to respond when given the chance. In the twenty-first century, the Foreign Office will remain excellent only if excellent women, ethnic minority, LGBTQ+, disabled, and lower socio-economic background candidates from places north of Watford and west of Reading get the same opportunities to progress as white, straight, middle class men from the south-east.

In a public institution in a status-quo power with constantly changing political leaders, muddling through was a way of life. Muddling through but striving incrementally to improve, just like people in Salford. I wanted everyone in the FCO to know they were doing worthwhile work, in an organisation that looked at all levels like the country it represented, and I wanted the organisation to maintain a global reputation for high-quality thinking. Bespoke leadership, connecting individually with everyone you lead, is best, but in a large organisation this is simply impossible. Contrary to Machiavelli's advice, I did not delegate the toughest messages. These days, leaders who are absent on the difficult days are found wanting; their lieutenants attract sympathy, not obloquy. The more difficult the message, the more important that the leader deliver it.

For most of my five years in the job, other (unplanned, unsought) work was more prominent (withdrawing from the EU, coping with coronavirus), but these lodestars were fixed at the start. Even though the most urgent regularly displaced the most important, I tried to return to the important as often as pressure from urgent work allowed. I strove to make the development and implementation of British foreign policy more coherent. From July 2016, four separate ministries were responsible for different aspects of UK foreign policy. In early 2020, DExEU disappeared, and in 2021, the FCO and DFID were merged (for the third time). DIT remains separate, with an existence more difficult to understand and justify after the negotiation and signing of the first raft of post-EU trade agreements (and no responsibility for trading relations with Europe, which still accounts for more than 40% of total UK foreign trade).

I tried to apply everything I had learned from Patrick, David, Jeremy, and all the great leaders I had worked for. I often failed. But returning to the example of good leaders can only help: they see the biggest picture; they do not allow themselves to get bogged down in the parochial; they do not disregard what is inconvenient or unfamiliar; they question their own most cherished views and accept evidence to support different points of view rather than look for constant reaffirmation of their existing views.

When I retired, I recalled a conversation thirty-odd years earlier with Stephen Egerton. We were flying between Jeddah and Riyadh when he asked why I wanted to be a British diplomat. My answer in 1987 was along the lines of: 'I'd rather play a small part in something big and worthwhile than a big part in something small and futile. In the end, I'd rather be a small fish in a big pond than a big fish in a small pond. Being small doesn't mean you can't make a difference.' I tried to make a difference.

It is possible (but rare) to get leadership wholly wrong; it is impossible to get it wholly right. In the end, other people judge success; public self-assessment is worthless. Those who love us are sadly inadequate assessors of our performance (but so, too, are those who dislike us). I hope, even suspect, that, if they were still alive, Monsignor Egan and K. C. Conroy would be generous.

11

Proposed Reforms for the Future of the UK

The death of the queen hit the United Kingdom like a freight train hitting a calf that has strayed onto the tracks. We now have time to take stock of the fundamentals of the UK: not only the monarchy but also Parliament and government.

In times past, such an agenda would have been referred to as a Royal Commission. Since the Second World War, twenty-five Royal Commissions have reported on subjects ranging from capital punishment to the National Health Service, but none has been set up this century. If a Royal Commission on the Constitution and Governance of the United Kingdom were empanelled, this chapter outlines what my submission would be.

When Tony Blair became prime minister, he joined permanent secretaries at their Wednesday morning meeting and told them that ideology would not drive his agenda in government – rather, he was interested in competence. He announced the end of the see-sawing of competing ideologies that had marked transfers of power since the Second World War: six years of the most radical Labour government succeeded by thirteen years of Conservatives, followed by six more years of Labour, four years of Conservatives, and five of Labour. The Thatcher/Major years were the most radical departure from previous administrations since Attlee came to power in 1945. After eighteen years, Mrs Thatcher's approach was not merely entrenched but also largely vindicated in the mind of the new prime minister. He told permanent secretaries that, when he faced re-election, he would invite the electorate to judge his Labour government by their competence in power rather than the purity of their pursuit of ideological goals. (Subsequent events proved that the country was more impressed by this approach than the Labour Party.)

In the last twenty years, the drive for competence has stalled. Politicians all talk about 're-setting' or 'getting back to basics'; if nothing else, leaving the EU is a chance to start afresh. For me, the malaise does not run deep; the fundamentals of the UK are strong. Over the last two centuries, despite the barracking at PMQs and anonymous nastiness of new media, life has become measurably better for everyone in the UK. In Washington in the 1990s, I met Gertrude Himmelfarb, the historian; over dinner she extolled the example of the United Kingdom. In the nineteenth century, the UK became more populous, more industrialised, and more urbanised. At the same time, British society became more law-abiding, better educated, and better represented in Parliament. Many other countries followed in Britain's footsteps, but the UK led the way and managed the transition in its own way, without internal revolution or external interference. The changes Himmelfarb charted were continued and consolidated in the twentieth century.

Over the same period, politics in the UK coalesced around a set of principles; despite the noise, contemporary political debate is about emphasis and nuance. I saw this every day at work but, because what we share is so much taken for granted, the common ground is rarely acknowledged, still less celebrated. Anyone who seeks to break this consensus may take over a political party (Michael Foot, Jeremy Corbyn) but will not in the end take over the country. Up close, it is clear that most British politicians agree that the key choice for voters is how well governments observe and implement these shared principles when in power: the government should protect and promote the freedom, safety, and security of the UK and its citizens at home and overseas; it should promote prosperity and equality of opportunity for its citizens; and it should protect the vulnerable, at home and overseas.

My reform agenda is about sprucing things up rather than challenging the fundamentals. I like the fundamentals: freedom, mutual respect, community, solidarity, kindness to strangers, openness to new talent, tolerance of 'the other'. Britons may live as they like as long as they do not harm others. Britons know that their key national institutions are ancient and tested in adversity; they are less aware that their robustness derives in part from their ability to adapt before changes they do not control sweep them away.

The foundation myth of any country requires it to be different from and usually better than any other. The UK has had so many moments in history that could be considered inceptions that no one agrees which was most important. In 927, Æthelstan was accepted as first king of the English.

In 1066, William the Conqueror provided England with one of only two truly memorable dates, according to Sellar and Yeatman. In 1215, the barons extracted Magna Carta from John and, in 1588, Elizabeth I saw off Philip II of Spain. When she died childless in 1603, her first cousin twice removed, James VI, united the thrones of Scotland and England; the union remained personal until the two parliaments amalgamated the countries in 1707. The United Kingdom of Great Britain and Ireland was established in 1801, becoming the United Kingdom of Great Britain and Northern Ireland when London recognised the Irish Free State in 1922. The last time the Royal coat of arms changed was in 1837, when Victoria succeeded her uncle William IV to the British throne but, because she was a woman, could not succeed to the throne of Hanover, which, applying the Salic law of succession, went to William's younger brother, Ernest Augustus.

When I was PUS, the Czech ambassador told me that he had fallen in love with the idea of Britain when studying here in the 1960s. Fifty years after first setting foot in London, he remembered handling British coins for the first time. Some of the pennies dated from the 1830s; he marvelled at the fact that they had been in circulation for longer than his country had existed, even as an aspiration. He pointed out that decimalisation had been one of the most radical events since then in the UK, whereas his country had undergone two revolutions, one violent, one 'velvet', and had split in two. He said, 'Constancy in everything important' is what distinguished the UK.

Despite a dozen regicides over the course of numerous civil wars, only one completely displaced the idea of monarchy, and the resulting Commonwealth lasted just eleven years in the seventeenth century. The king or (for 134 of the last 185 years) the queen has always been a focal point of the idea of Britain. Popular perceptions, particularly of Victoria and Elizabeth II, have come – in an inarticulate but rooted way – to represent the country's view of itself: dutiful, faithful, principled, calm, and kind. When he was trying to sum up the UK and why it was still worth international attention, Douglas Hurd would list aspects of the national character; his list looked like mine. In a conversation long ago, he cast about for a one-word summary and could do no better than 'decency'. If one person embodied that quietly confident virtue, it was the queen.

In a rooted country, which downplays the importance of its rare revolutions, leaders sense they will not get far couching their ideas in revolutionary terms. They seek to build on what is already there, to reconnect with the flair and energy (and success) of earlier times. They present themselves, even if they do not acknowledge it, as custodians. But sixty years after Dean Acheson's taunt that the UK had lost an empire but failed to find a new role, all institutions need refurbishment, even if the language of change has to stress comforting continuity.

My starting point is that the fundamentals are sound: the monarchy, first-past-the-post parliamentary democracy, the common law and independent judiciary, equal treatment and equal opportunity, an education system that stresses good basic standards for all while unapologetically offering excellence for the most able. The problem is that everything built on those fundamentals needs an overhaul.

Monarchy

As the first British sovereign to celebrate her Platinum Jubilee, Elizabeth II was first to acknowledge that a change of reign was imminent. In Charles III's reign, the House of Windsor needs to be small (an intention signalled, perhaps, when just seven family members appeared with the queen on the balcony of Buckingham Palace on 5 June 2022). For a transitional period, Princess Anne and the Wessexes might continue their royal duties, but all others should retire.

In the model of monarchy I propose, a working royal family reduced in size would be matched by a reduction in royal titles. Royal titles can be withdrawn without dishonour: in earlier times, princesses surrendered their 'HRH' on marriage; a noble title for life might be substituted. King George V attempted the reform. Meghan Markle joined the royal family just as those reforms – which foresaw that only one great grandchild (the direct heir) of a reigning monarch would be HRH – were about to bite. In future, going further than George V envisaged, only the monarch's children and the heir's heir might be HRH. Courtesy titles, even where more senior than baron, could be for life only (so no more hereditary titles would be created).

With Charles III on the throne, with these changes in place, the royal family might be just five people: king, queen, the prince and princess of Wales, and Prince George. The royal family would be explicitly and exclusively British. During Elizabeth II's reign, eighteen realms became republics; the fourteen remaining realms might be encouraged to re-examine their status. In the middle of the twenty-first century, an absentee head of state – without the strong ties of familiarity and long service the queen enjoyed – is hard to understand, let alone defend. The Commonwealth would remain.

Royal residences should also reduce in number. Buckingham Palace, Windsor Castle, the Palace of Holyroodhouse, and Balmoral would be the core. Kensington Palace, Clarence House, and St James's Palace would be available for other public uses. Sandringham might be sold. The new king's personal interest in Highgrove would postpone consideration of its future until the next reign.

With a smaller royal family, the calls on the time of individual royals might be greater. Under Charles III, the practice initiated by George VI of the monarch's contact with the cabinet being principally (almost solely) via the prime minister might be re-examined. The new king might revert to a pattern of regular (if not frequent) contact with a range of senior cabinet ministers (chancellor, foreign secretary, home secretary, and perhaps others). The quantity, and therefore type, of other work would be cut back. The work overseas of senior royals (basically, the smaller group proposed) is invaluable for the country; the benefit of overseas programmes for other royals has been reducing for some time. New arrangements would largely codify existing practice.

The honours system should be updated, while reconnecting with its original purposes. The system recognises service to the monarch and latterly service to the state. The Order of St Michael and St George was established in 1818 to recognise specific service in the eastern Mediterranean.

It quickly expanded to become the order that recognised service overseas, mostly official work. In 1967, the Foreign Office employed sixty-seven ambassadors who were KCMGs ('sirs'). In 2022, four ambassadors are dames; no career ambassador is sir* (but one member of the FCDO Board in London is). In the 1990s, the idea took root that no one should be honoured simply because of the job they did. These days, an honour is still part of the package for only a small number of public servants. Cabinet ministers are all automatically members of the Privy Council, because constitutionally the cabinet is a committee of the Privy Council. High court judges are knighted automatically on appointment. I believe that is correct. Some jobs are open only to people who have already achieved a certain distinction. By definition, judges, generals, senior ambassadors, and senior civil servants are doing work of such importance to the government that their work can be recognised at the beginning of their tenure; the state has an interest in signalling its confidence in their quality.

In the law, honours also explicitly compensate for a reduction in salary: KCs who become judges invariably take a substantial cut in pay. As young people contemplate career options, in times past they knew that, although choosing a career in public service would not make them rich, they could receive other recognition from the state. This automatic bestowal still applies to judges because no one wants ministers to decide which judges deserve a

---

* In 2022, two political appointee ambassadors are Lord Llewellyn of Steep OBE PC (in Rome) and Sir George Hollingbery KCMG (in Havana).

rationed honour; the idea that ministers would withhold an honour from a judge whose judgements they disliked does not appeal. I would treat other senior public servants like senior judges and return to the system of knighthoods and damehoods for permanent secretaries, three- and four-star military officers and senior ambassadors.

King George V established the Order of the British Empire in 1917, when the British Empire covered one quarter of the world's land surface. The concept of 'empire' is now problematic for many potential recipients of awards; indeed, a number decline the honour because of its name. 'Empire' might be exchanged for 'Excellence'. If that were done, the long name of the Order would also need to change from 'The Most Excellent Order...', perhaps to 'The Most Outstanding Order of British Excellence'.

The orders celebrating the greatest achievements need to look more like the country as a whole. Over ten years, the Orders of the Garter, Thistle, Merit, and Companions of Honour might all become 50:50 men and women.

The medals and badges themselves might be made the same for men and women, the same size and worn in the same way. I have never understood Queen Mary's objection to women wearing neck decorations, when many more women than men wear necklaces.

Prime Minister

The prime minister enjoys greater powers than any monarch since Henry VIII. And no one can oblige him to share these powers, as Nick Clegg discovered during the coalition government. Between 2010 and 2015, the star chamber (PM, DPM, chancellor, and chief secretary to the Treasury) may have provided strategic direction and taken some big decisions, but in practice David Cameron decided much that never made it to the star chamber's agenda. The PM controls all appointments in the public service, including senior military, diplomatic, and Church of England appointments; they control most of the honours system (but not the two oldest orders of chivalry, the Order of Merit or the Royal Victorian Order, whose total membership is less than 2% of all award holders); they control all ministerial appointments. And they actively exercise these powers over everyone around them. Lack of security in senior office for those in close proximity is a phenomenon Cardinal Wolsey or Thomas Cromwell would recognise.

Prime ministerial powers have grown steadily since Robert Walpole was the king's first minister to be known by the title. The position was not acknowledged in law and the order of precedence until 1905 (when Campbell-Bannerman was placed immediately after the archbishop of York; among cabinet ministers, he is still formally outranked by the lord chancellor, who ranks immediately before the archbishop of York). For most of the last three hundred years, the prime minister's office in Downing Street was small. Its size reflected the role, chairing cabinet but leaving secretaries of state to run their departments; line ministries had the bulk of the staff because they took most of the decisions. The Cabinet Office served the whole of cabinet and the system of cabinet committees, many of which were not chaired by the prime minister; it was explicitly not the prime minister's office.

In 2010, the CRAG put the Civil Service on a statutory footing for the first time. I believe the same needs to be done for the prime minister. In the absence of an act setting out the PM's power, the presumption has grown in the system that, where there is a lack of clarity or an issue arises for the first time, the PM decides, usually without reference to anyone else.

Outside advisers have always been a feature of central government. In earlier times, their position was regularised with a peerage and a formal government job (for example, Beaverbrook in the First World War). A PM's press secretary often came from Fleet Street (Joe Haines for Wilson, Bernard Ingham for Thatcher) but not always (Donald Maitland for Heath, Gus O'Donnell and Christopher Meyer for Major). In the 1980s, these outsiders began to be called special advisers (SpAds) and to become a fixed part of the machinery. The CRAG also set rules for SpAds.

While Downing Street has limited the number of SpAds elsewhere in Whitehall, they have proliferated inside Number 10. Every attic and cellar in the building is now occupied; nobody, apart from the PM, has their own office. Over time, SpAds have begun to resemble the *cabinet* of a French minister; they have become the group to which a minister turns first and on whom they rely most. Because their tenure depends explicitly on their boss remaining in office, they are felt to be most loyal. As a group, they are becoming large and ambitious enough not to need the rest of the ministry, except when things go wrong. Clearer rules, a clearer understanding of the boundaries between work undertaken by SpAds and civil servants, and smaller numbers would make the system work better.

Cabinet

The cabinet, too, needs reform. The wall behind the dais in Committee Room 14 of the House of Commons is dominated by a large, gloomy painting of Gladstone's second cabinet. It depicts fifteen men. At the end of the nineteenth century, when the UK was indisputably the most powerful country in the world, the cabinet was never larger than eighteen (unpaid) men. In the twentieth century, the cabinet has grown. The Ministerial and Other Salaries Act (1975) stipulates that there may be no more than eighty-three paid ministers at any one time, excluding the lord chancellor, three law officers, and twenty-two government whips.

Although the number of cabinet salaries is fixed at twenty-one, the cabinet is always larger. The core cabinet may include as full members ministers who do not draw a salary for their cabinet work (typically, the party chairperson). The right to attend cabinet meetings is extended to other ministers, at the discretion of the prime minister. In Boris Johnson's cabinets, this group was never smaller than five and at one point was as large as ten.

The cabinet is too large to be an effective part of government. Group dynamics matter. The European Union is still recovering from the expansion from fifteen to twenty-eight (then twenty-seven) attendees at its meetings. The

UN Security Council is at the margin of effectiveness with fifteen members. When more than fifteen are at the table, the chair finds it more difficult to include all participants to the extent they want to be included and keep sessions under three hours long (I never attended a meeting in which the fourth hour felt as if it added anything useful). Consequently, the chair exercises (even) more power, choosing who will intervene and when, and gavelling agenda items to a conclusion. Other participants see what is happening, grumble (even if not loudly) and feel less bound by the meeting's decisions.

Cabinet meetings should be half their current size. Those invited because the PM feels bad about not offering them a ministry should not be invited. And those who attend in a political capacity should not be invited. Mrs Thatcher was the first prime minister habitually to include the chief whip and chair of the party in her cabinet (the latter as either paymaster-general or chancellor of the duchy of Lancaster). In times past, political cabinets existed separately from cabinet: the cabinet secretary would withdraw and party officials arrive, and discussion would change from the merits of a policy to how it would be framed to the party in Parliament and the country. Latterly, the difference between the two types of meeting has become blurred, because office holders who would have previously attended only political cabinet are now full cabinet members.

Ministries should be overhauled and consolidated. In the 2020s, it is not clear what useful function separate secretaries of state for Northern Ireland, Scotland, and Wales fulfil. All three nations have their own parliament/assembly. Such residual functions as require representation at the cabinet table could be undertaken by one person (perhaps a secretary of state for the Union). Ministries dealing with the economy might be recast. Germany provides one model: in Chancellor Scholz's coalition, Robert Habeck combines the handling of the economy with climate change. One ministry might look after all overseas affairs.

Cabinet ministers should also be given greater certainty of tenure. A prime minister at the start of a new administration might announce that the new cabinet is expected to serve the full term of the Parliament, explicitly foregoing the routine reshuffle that has been a regular feature of British politics since Macmillan's Night of the Long Knives in 1962. In Germany, after a government is formed and the president swears in a new cabinet (Scholz's has nineteen members), its members are expected to serve the full four years of the Bundestag. Occasionally, ministers resign; even more rarely, they are sacked. In the UK, the average incumbency for a cabinet minister other than the prime minister is less than three years. In the five-and-a-half years she was permanent secretary at the Department for Digital, Culture, Media and Sport (DCMS), Sue Owen had six different secretaries of state. The fact that cabinet ministers know that the PM has their P45 in his or her back pocket seriously inhibits the openness of discussion. Only the most confident or insensitive cabinet minister has no fear of the next cabinet reshuffle (generally, less than eighteen months' distant).

Part of the rebalancing with prime ministerial powers would be to return to secretaries of state the power of appointment within their department. Until the middle of the twentieth century, secretaries of states chose their own junior ministers rather than accepting the PM's decision. They should get that power back. When Jack Straw was appointed foreign secretary in 2001, he chose his own parliamentary private secretary (PPS). Even though it is unpaid, a PPS job is traditionally viewed as an early, essential step on the road to a ministerial career. Its function is to be a secretary of state's eyes and ears in Parliament. The personal link between secretary of state and PPS is key to a successful working relationship; PPSs who do well are commended by their bosses to the PM. In 2022, the prime minister chooses PPSs for their whole ministerial team; a secretary of state can make a case for a particular backbench MP, but in the end they must accept the prime minister's choice. I would also return this patronage to secretaries of state.

Junior Ministers

Junior ministers, too, are too numerous. The *Economist* once estimated that the UK could claim one quarter of the world's complement of junior ministers. The UK has too many, serving too short a time, in too many layers. The first minister of state was appointed in the Second World War; the experiment was not repeated until 1950 (for the Foreign Office) but quickly became entrenched. The UK is one of the few countries with two levels of junior ministers plus extra gradations in the whips' office. The payroll (those 108 salaried ministers, law officers, and whips) are the bedrock of a prime minister's support in Parliament; someone to whom you give a job and who relies on you to remain in that job is most likely to be loyal. Sometimes the promise of a more interesting future job is enough to win someone's loyalty. The web of prime ministerial patronage is extensive, but not extensive enough for some prime ministers. In recent years, envoys for everything from trade with a particular country to discrete policy areas (be it girls' education or post-Holocaust issues) have proliferated. In 2022, Boris Johnson appointed a Deputy Special Envoy for Freedom of Religion or Belief: the ladder of ministerial promotion is proving extendable at the bottom. In theory, giving a job turns the recipient into a supporter.

In practice, the most able junior ministers have a frustrating time. In law, most departmental decisions are reserved for the secretary of state. Time as a junior minister is a desirable (but not essential) apprenticeship for MPs wanting to get into cabinet. I never met a junior minister who had not progressed to cabinet who felt they had enjoyed a fulfilling ministerial career.

Surveying the scene, an ambitious new MP can plot their course through the strata of political seniority: PPS through the whip's office, to PUSS (parliamentary under-secretary of state) to minister of state, to cabinet minister, to a great office of state, to prime minister. John Major managed all steps in less than ten years, becoming PPS to Sir Patrick Mayhew in January 1981 and topping out as prime minister in November 1990.

I propose just one grade of junior minister with their

overall number pruned. No department need have more than one junior minister in the Lords; some departments could share a Lords' minister. No department need have more than four junior ministers in total.

House of Lords

Since becoming a peer in 2021, I have learned that lords are among the most enthusiastic supporters of Lords' reform. It seems that only people who aspire to become members of the House of Lords want to keep things as they are. The incomplete reform of 1999 has left the house more bloated and less legitimate than ever. The easiest course is to do nothing. The present set-up clearly works to the satisfaction of the people who, if really dissatisfied, could shake things up. It could persist for a long time: one lesson of diplomacy is 'nothing is so durable as an unsatisfactory status quo'.

Not all democracies feel the need to have a second chamber: for example, all Scandinavian countries, New Zealand, and Israel are unicameral, in the case of Sweden, Norway, Denmark, and New Zealand having previously been bicameral. In all parliaments, the second/upper chamber is in modern times junior to the lower chamber, which in general has acquired principal or exclusive responsibility for raising money. Tenure of members is generally longer in the upper house than in the lower house and, even where the membership is wholly elected, not all members stand for election simultaneously – so there is greater stability and continuity in membership. Nearly everywhere, the upper chamber is a revising chamber, a place for reflection and second thoughts, a repository of experience and expertise.

Given the fact that a two-chamber system has been a feature of the British Parliament since 1341 and that many countries have happily copied this model, I assume that a second chamber will continue to be a feature of the UK Parliament.

The present set-up has advantages that a reformed House would benefit from keeping, and which potential reformers may fear would be lost in any reform. The iron-clad courtesy of the Lords distinguishes it from most other legislative chambers in the world. The fact that members enjoy the highest honour of public life means that a certain sort of ambition has been satisfied; Lords are not as susceptible to a fear of missing out on future preferment, which means they are less likely to be corrupt. They do not have to limit their interventions to the areas where they are felt (or feel themselves) expert. Contributions are diverse; the set-piece debates are high quality.

Any proposal for reform must actively seek to preserve these strengths. But fear of spoiling what is good should not deter reformers. Glaring defects must be tackled. Hereditary privilege has no place in any modern democratic legislature. The voice of the state religion cannot be the only voice of religion heard there. Its membership cannot be large (one quarter larger than the elected house) and infinitely expandable. Notoriously, it is the second largest legislative assembly in the world after the Congress of the

People's Republic of China, which represents 1.3 billion people.

In surveys, British voters express dissatisfaction with the House of Lords: over 60% of respondents to YouGov's tracking poll consistently say they have either no confidence or little confidence in the House of Lords; only 2% say they have a lot of confidence. But most voters give the Lords only scant attention. The House relies on the low level of outside interest in how it works to preserve the indefensible. At some stage, the outside world will intrude. Institutions in need of reform always enjoy the experience more when they take charge of the reform themselves.

Although the case for reform is compelling, I foresee immediate opposition to my proposals from within the existing House of Lords. Most members will be personally and disagreeably affected. They will find many aspects to criticise, not least the suggestion of two types of peer in a reformed House. But vested interests must be confronted.

From the Bryce Commission (1918) to the Burns Report (2017) proposals for Lords' reform have usually emerged from a committee, with more than a whiff of unhappy compromise. My proposals draw on their work and the work of many others, from Roger Sherman and the framers of the US Constitution to Billy Bragg. I believe they are a coherent package, but every element could be negotiated and changed in detail. Some elements could be dropped while leaving the remaining package worthwhile.

My proposals strive to accommodate three fundamental principles – the three principles that must be central to any effort at comprehensive reform:

- First, that a reformed House of Lords must respect the primacy of the House of Commons in the UK legislature;
- Second, that the relative importance of the two chambers must be reflected in their size;
- Third, the fact that all chambers in a legislature need legitimacy in the eyes of the electorate.

I assume that legitimacy requires a connection to the electorate, even an indirect one, and that membership better reflecting the country as a whole would help increase legitimacy. I also assume that the privileges of a life peerage, including an existing life peerage, are not sacrosanct and do not necessarily include membership of the House of Lords until a life peer is prepared to retire. After the reform, as now, the titles 'Lord' and 'Baroness' would be for life, but membership of the legislature would not.

To reduce the size of the House, I propose three things, all of which would be implemented over time: first, to remove excepted hereditary peers; second, to limit service to twenty years; and third, to reduce the number of bishops.

The case for removing the remaining hereditary peers is easiest to make. The presence in the legislature of people (overwhelmingly men) who are members entirely because of the achievements of their ancestors has long been controversial. The controversy has not resulted in action for three main reasons: first, it suits the House of Commons for the House of Lords to be demonstrably less democratic because, as long as that is the case, the Commons' primacy will not be challenged; second, those benefiting personally have been able to use the labyrinthine rules of the House to fend off attacks on their position; and third, reform of the House, even for ministers who enthusiastically embrace the cause, has never been sufficiently high a priority for a government to organise to overcome that self-serving defence.

Everyone in the House acknowledges that the reform of 1999 was supposed to be a temporary stage on the way to a more comprehensive reform. The single strangest aspect of the 1999 reform was the preserving of ninety-two places for hereditary peers. Robert Salisbury has entertained readers of the *Financial Times* with his account of how he, as leader of the opposition in the House of Lords, bamboozled the Labour government into accepting so large a number, which would then regenerate itself. Twenty-odd years later the elections to replace retired or deceased excepted hereditaries have descended into farce. Bruce Grocott entertains the House with a dissection of these elections each time a result is announced.

I took part in two by-elections in 2021. The first was to replace the Countess of Mar on her retirement. After the 1999 reform, the Countess remained in the House as one of fifteen hereditary peers serving as deputy speakers. Whenever one of these fifteen retires, the group in which she or he sat votes to choose a replacement. The Journal Office at the House of Lords maintains the list of hereditary peers eligible to stand and organises the by-elections. Peers elected in by-elections become members of the House of Lords until death or retirement. Because the Countess was a crossbencher, all 190 crossbench peers were eligible voters.

The convenor of the crossbenchers organised hustings. Initially, ten male hereditary peers declared an interest in running (the Journal Office's register runs to 202 eligible candidates, only one of whom is a woman). Because of the pandemic, the hustings took place over Zoom. Because he did not own a computer, the nonagenarian candidate dropped out. The wife of one of the octogenarian candidates took a dim view of her husband's ambition; he, too, failed to appear at the hustings.

In the end, eight men took part. In the modern way, the moderator put identical questions to all candidates, who also made short opening and closing statements. Even though we had only one hour, answers were revealing. One candidate came completely unstuck (in other words, was unable to articulate any kind of reply) when asked, 'Why should we vote for you?' Another found it difficult to explain why we should vote for him when he had previously stood for Conservative, Liberal Democrat, and Labour vacancies. Three more thought that there was no need for further reform, either because 'the hereditaries have already done their bit' or 'most members don't turn up, so the size of the House isn't really an issue'. For me, the choice was therefore whittled down to two. We had almost no other information to guide us: manifestos are required to run to less than 100 words. In the end, I voted for the younger candidate, because the average age of members of the House is seventy-one, and age diversity seems desirable.

I could not bring myself to vote in the whole-House election to replace a Conservative hereditary; information on the candidates was too sparse for any to seem deserving of a place in the legislature. I noted later that the candidate commended by the Conservative whips prevailed.

My second election was voting to replace the late Viscount Simon, a Labour peer. Three men ran. One announced himself at the outset as a Conservative. This was honest but curious: the Carter Convention requires peers to respect the balance in 1999 between the political groupings in the House; a retiring Labour peer must therefore be replaced by a new Labour peer. Despite the convention, the Conservative attracted 10% of the vote. A second had sat in the House until 1997 as a Conservative before crossing the floor to Labour, but he was now in his eighties. The third was someone whose image on the internet was generally sporting a Liberal Democrat rosette. The eighty-three-year-old ex-Conservative now sits again in the House, slightly increasing the average age of its membership.

The era when peers had a continuing role in the administration of the area which gave them their title, where usually they had large estates, is several centuries in the past. If any hereditary peer's personal service is outstanding enough to deserve appointment as a peer, fair enough: they can be given a life peerage like anyone else.

Two of the excepted hereditaries occupy hereditary great offices of state: the earl marshal (since 1672, always the Duke of Norfolk) and the lord great chamberlain (since the eighteenth century, rotating between members of the Cholmondeley, Willoughby, and Carrington families, it being the Marquess of Cholmondeley in the reign of Elizabeth II). A leave of absence has not prevented Lord Cholmondeley from fulfilling his duties at the State Opening of Parliament.

Both he and the Duke of Norfolk could continue to fulfil their ceremonial duties without being members of the House.

I propose that Parliament and the government accept Bruce Grocott's proposals to end, immediately, by-elections for excepted hereditary vacancies. From the day the reform became law, there would be no more excepted hereditary by-elections. Ten years after that day, any excepted hereditary members who had not already left, having completed twenty years' service, would leave the House, as the upper limit of membership came down to its intended long-term size. Reducing the House, over time, by ninety-two is a start but still leaves membership over 700.

People argue endlessly about the 'correct' or 'ideal' size of a reformed House of Lords; most agree that it should be smaller than the elected House (itself one of the largest legislatures in the world). In 2017, Terry Burns suggested 600 in his report on the size of the House, 600 being the nearest round number smaller than the Commons' 650. My pitch is more ambitious, arguing for a House of 400 members, that is, about half its current strength and 40% smaller than the Commons. This revives a proposal made by Lord Rosebery in his report of 1908.

The House needs to be more effective. By making it significantly smaller, it can also be significantly cheaper. I propose that the reduction take place over ten years, with about 150 peers leaving the House immediately as the reform comes into force and a further 250 (net) leaving over the following ten years. When the reform is fully implemented, the House would achieve the final size of 400.

There is no easy way to cull 300 life peers, even if the cull takes place over time. Any method would be controversial and exclude some of the most effective members of the House. But I believe the need for reform overrides individual claims to continued membership; to maximise acceptance, any method of cutting needs to be consistently applied. I propose that life peers retire after twenty years' membership of the Lords; 205 life peers would be immediately affected.

To soften the blow, I propose that a group of those who would otherwise retire should remain in the House until full implementation, ten years after the reform begins. Symbolically, I pluck the number ninety-two from the ether, mirroring the number of excepted hereditaries who stayed on after the 1999 reform. Before the act came into force, the 205 life peers immediately affected plus the 100 life peers and fifty-four excepted hereditaries who would be due to retire by the middle of 2027 would take part in a whole-House election to choose ninety-two who would stay on until the end of the transition. When any of the ninety-two died or retired, they would not be replaced.

All departing peers would be paid a pension, whose size would reflect the length of their service in the Lords, perhaps £1,000 per year for each year of service, with a maximum pension of £20,000. They would also continue to enjoy certain privileges as ex-members – perhaps a more generous package of continued access to the palace and administrative support than retired peers receive now.

To repeat, I acknowledge that many able and, indeed, beloved members of the House would depart. Although they would remain peers of the realm, the House would lose their experience and memory in its day-to-day business. There is no disguising the negative impact on the work of the House as well as the preferences of serving peers. But I can see no more compelling a way to reduce membership. One further advantage from the point of the view of the Conservative government is that, by putting a ceiling of twenty years on service, the bulge of Labour appointments at the start of Tony Blair's first government would leave.

A third category of peer that would also be affected by a comprehensive reform is the bishops' bench. At present, twenty-six bishops are members of the House of Lords, all Anglican; five serve by virtue of the see they hold (the two English archbishops plus the bishops of London, Durham, and Winchester); the rest take their seat by seniority, retiring at the age of seventy. In a House shedding half its membership, the bishops might make a disproportionately large contribution: among 400 peers, there would be ten bishops, including the five who have traditionally been members of the House. After the reform was implemented, no new bishops would be admitted apart from the five who have automatic right of entry, until the overall number of bishops in the Lords had fallen to ten. If that process had not been completed by the ten-year mark, the longest serving 'excess' would retire in order to get it down to ten.

The effect of these measures would be to reduce the size of the House by about 250 immediately, by about 400 in 2027 (that is, five years into the reform), and by 530 by 2032. Membership of the House would, of course, need to be refreshed during the ten years. I propose that a maximum of twelve life peers be created each year of the transition: six government, three opposition, and three crossbench. By the beginning of 2033, membership would be just under 400.

But bloated size is not the greatest of the Lords' challenges. Right now, members have precisely zero democratic legitimacy. If the reform ended with reducing numbers in the way I suggest, then every single peer would owe their appointment to David Cameron and his successors as prime minister. Not acceptable.

The key role of the House of Lords is revising legislation, much of which passes the Commons with minimal scrutiny. Successive governments have acknowledged that the Lords have consistently improved their legislation. Changes are made in committee and after debate on the floor of the House; there are relatively few votes.

I propose two types of members of the House of Lords: those able to vote and those able to take part in all proceedings of the House except voting. Non-voting members of the Lords would be able to serve on committees and as deputy speakers. The country has coped with the concept of different sorts of peer since the Middle Ages, when five ranks of peer emerged: duke, marquess, earl, viscount, and baron.

My first principle is to guarantee the primacy of the House of Commons, so I do not propose a separate election to decide which peers have the right to vote. Rather, at each general election, there would be a shadow election in the background which would determine which peers had voting rights for the period of the Parliament being elected.

In the first general election after the reform was enacted and at all subsequent general elections, voters would continue to have one vote, for their constituency MP. But their vote would count a second time to decide voting peers. I propose dividing the UK into ten regions; each region would return twenty peers, according to party strengths in that region. Each region would be treated in the same way. But the population of each region would vary widely. Northern Ireland, Scotland, and Wales would each be a region. England would be divided into seven: Greater London, South East, South West, East of England, Midlands, North West, and North East. The effect would be to push representation and power to the three other nations and away from the South East of England: the two regions of Greater London and South East would have a combined population of twenty million but the same number of voting peers as Northern Ireland and Wales with a combined population of five million.

Four of the ten regions are existing administrative units: Scotland, Wales, Northern Ireland, and Greater London. The other six English regions would be of similar population size to each other (but significantly bigger than Scotland, Wales, and Northern Ireland and somewhat smaller than London) apart from South East, which would be approximately one-third larger. The boundaries of regions would follow existing county lines. North West would comprise Cheshire, Cumbria, Greater Manchester, Lancashire, and Merseyside. North East would comprise County Durham, Humberside, North Yorkshire, Northumberland, South Yorkshire, Tyne and Wear, and West Yorkshire. Midlands would comprise Derbyshire, Shropshire, Staffordshire, Warwickshire, West Midlands, and Worcestershire. East of England would comprise Cambridgeshire, Leicestershire, Lincolnshire, Norfolk, Northamptonshire, Nottinghamshire, Rutland, and Suffolk. South West would comprise Bristol, Cornwall, Devon, Dorset, Gloucestershire, Herefordshire, Somerset, and Wiltshire. South East would be Bedfordshire, Berkshire, Buckinghamshire, East Sussex, Essex, Hampshire, Hertfordshire, Isle of Wight, Kent, Oxfordshire, Surrey, and West Sussex.

The threshold for securing one voting peer would be 5% of the vote in a particular region. 'Hangover' seats (those remaining when all blocks of 5% had been distributed) would be decided within each region according to the following formula: the first unassigned seat would go to the biggest party in the region, the second to the second biggest party, the third again to the biggest party. On the rare occasion that there was a fourth unassigned seat, that would go to the third biggest party. The distribution of unassigned seats would explicitly favour the largest parties in the region. Parties that failed to secure 5% in a region would not be eligible for any seats in that final reckoning. In advance of the general election, all parties would provide candidate lists, so voters would know who might be the voting peers representing their region. All parties would be obliged to nominate existing peers before nominating anyone who was not a peer. In compiling their lists, parties would be required to alternate men and women, placing a woman in first place.

The bigger parties (Conservative, Labour, and Liberal

1 Northern Ireland
2 Scotland
3 Wales
4 North West
5 North East
6 Midlands
7 East of England
8 South West
9 South East
10 Greater London

Democrats) would be able to fill all slots with a realistic prospect of election on candidate lists with existing peers. Because no party would be expected to secure more than 60% of the vote in any one region, parties would nominate a maximum of twelve candidates for each region; smaller parties might choose to nominate fewer.

Before any new peer was created for any party, all its existing life peers would have to be seated in the new

Parliament, which might mean existing peers transferring to represent a different region from the one where they were a candidate (something similar happens in federal elections in Germany). For example, the Green Party has two life peers, Baroness Bennett of Manor Castle and Baroness Jones of Moulsecoomb. They might both run on the Green Party list for their home area of Greater London. If, say, the Greens secured only one seat in London, whoever was top of the London list would represent London and the other would transfer to a different region where the Greens had cleared the 5% hurdle.

Candidates for the House of Commons would not be permitted to be candidates on the Lords lists in the same general election.

In advance of the election, the House of Lords Appointments Commission (HOLAC) would vet proposed peers in its usual way. They would vet only candidates with a realistic prospect of being elected; 'realistic prospect' would be guided by that party's historic general election performance. So, if the Monster Raving Loony Party nominated twelve peers in all ten regions, the Commission need not vet any of them. Anyone who was already a peer would pass muster by definition; others would be subject to the checks HOLAC already applies. In a direct election, voters can choose whomever they want (Bobby Sands won the by-election for Fermanagh and South Tyrone in April 1981 while serving a life sentence in Maze Prison). But, in an indirect or shadow election, some potential candidates with, for example, a criminal record, would be excluded.

Parties would give their candidate lists to HOLAC twelve

months before a scheduled general election to allow the Commission to do its work; they would publish lists on the same day as they formally nominate candidates to be MPs. Voters in all regions would therefore know before casting their single vote who their potential voting peers from all parties would be for their region.

'Elected' peers would serve for the whole of a Parliament, even if that took them beyond the normal ceiling of twenty years' service; peers who had breached the twenty-year limit would not be permitted to stand in the following general election. If an 'elected' peer died in office, they would be replaced by an existing peer; if the deceased peer belonged to a party that had no other peers in the chamber, then a crossbench volunteer would be sought to accept that party's whip for the balance of the Parliament. 'Elected' peers would be expected to work full time at the House of Lords. Unlike now, they would be salaried, with a salary fixed (symbolically) at 5% less than that for an MP. Other members of the House of Lords would continue to receive the allowance they get at present, because they would be working on the same terms as at present.

Part of the new system would, explicitly, be the creation of new peers chosen by voters in a general election. That would be most obvious after the first election under the new system. For example, the Scottish National Party does not nominate peers. But, if they performed as strongly as they did in the last election, they would have ten voting peers in the reformed House of Lords. Having created this batch (all of whom would be members for twenty years) the same batch would run in poll positions at the next election.

If this system had applied at the last election, it would have required offering fewer than thirty new peerages, a modest number compared with usual practice in the first year of a new Parliament. Sinn Féin would have been entitled to five; if they continue to reject the idea of taking part in a 'foreign' parliament, the peerages they won would not be created, reducing the overall number of voting peers.

The new House would be smaller; Scotland, Wales, Northern Ireland, and the English regions would play a greater part; women would play a greater part; and smaller parties would potentially play a greater part. If the reform had been in place in 2019, out of 200 'elected' peers, the Conservatives would have won eighty-five, Labour sixty-seven, Liberal Democrats fifteen, SNP ten, DUP eight, Sinn Féin five, Alliance three, Brexit two, SDLP two, UUP two, and Plaid Cymru one. Although the Greens won 2.61% of the national vote, it was evenly distributed across England, and they failed to clear the 5% hurdle in any region. The Brexit Party, on the other hand, won 2.01% of the national vote, concentrated in the North and Wales; they would have secured one seat in the North East and one in Wales.

In addition to 200 'elected' peers, twenty crossbenchers would also have voting rights. This group would be salaried in the same way as other voting peers and expected to work full time on Lords' business. Crossbenchers would vote among themselves as to who among them would have voting rights in a given Parliament; there would be a new vote at each general election. By convention, crossbench peers do not block government business in ping-pong votes; that convention would be reinforced, requiring crossbench peers to support the government in ping-pong votes. In effect, the twenty crossbench voting peers would be a bonus bloc for the government of the day (something similar applies in Italy's Senate).

In the reformed House of Lords, a government would rarely enjoy a majority of voting peers, because few British single-party governments get close to 50% of the popular vote (a reminder of the limits of their popular mandate). But any government in the new system would have a larger percentage of peers than any government since 1999. Before then, in a largely hereditary House, the Conservative majority was so entrenched that Labour governments only half-heartedly tried to challenge it. For their part, Conservative peers allowed Labour governments to get their key business through the House in the knowledge that if they became a persistent obstacle, they would likely be abolished.

Necessary new creations after a general election might push membership over the 400 limit. After the ten-year transition period, a moratorium on new peerages would be put in place until membership (by retirements or death) had fallen to 390.

UK governments have from time to time appointed ministers who were not already members of the legislature. Traditionally, in the UK, ministers have been either MPs or peers. It is easier (and the outcome more certain) to appoint a new minister to the Lords than to arrange a by-election in the Commons. In a smaller House of Lords, the government would not necessarily have scope to offer a peerage to a new minister. Part of the reform would be to allow a prime minister to appoint whomever they felt was best qualified for ministerial office without insisting that all choices be members either of the Commons or Lords. Standing orders would be altered to allow ministers who were not members of either House to be questioned and held accountable at the bar of either House. Cabinet ministers would continue to be privy counsellors.

In the fully reformed House, under the ceiling of 400 members, prime ministers would still be able to nominate new (non-voting) members of the House of Lords. The mix would be similar to how it is now, that is to say, peers for both public service and political service, which would also (as now) include peerages for members of political parties not in government.

The PM would remain responsible for political appointments (what used to be called 'working peers'); HOLAC would immediately assume sole responsibility for nominating public service peers. Both the Commission and the prime minister might be given a veto over each other's proposals. Over time, given the fact that all members of the House would retire after twenty years' service, about twenty new peers would be created each non-election year, at a ratio of three political peers for every one nominated for public service. From the point of full implementation of the reform, the proportion of new creations among the parties would reflect the national percentage of votes parties had received at the previous general election. A party that received 40% of the national vote in a general election would receive twenty-four of the sixty political peerages created over the following four years.

The Commission would be explicitly tasked with making

the House more representative of the country as a whole, by gender, region, ethnicity, disability, and socio-economic background. Crossbench peers would also include representatives of faiths other than Anglicanism. In the new House, 100 places would be reserved for crossbench peers (which would approximately maintain the existing percentage). Anglican bishops, as now, would be a separate group from the crossbenchers.

The House of Lords' powers would not change. It would continue (as has been the case since 1911) to play no part in agreeing finance bills; it would continue to observe the Salisbury Convention, not opposing the second or third reading of any government legislation set out in its election manifesto. As proposed in the Wakeham Report of 2000, the reformed House would retain a 'suspensory veto' – the power to delay, but not to block, a bill approved by the Commons in two successive parliamentary sessions. But, with the extra legitimacy conferred by the 'shadow' election, it would expect the House of Commons to weigh its interventions more seriously. In the eight years up to 2020, 360 private members bills were tabled in the House of Lords; just three made it to the statute book. That would change. I realise that the last sentence is a pious hope, but it is not an unreasonable expectation.

Civil Service

Since the 1850s, an impartial and professional civil service, recruited and promoted on merit, has served the UK well. In a survey of civil services around the world in 2017, the UK was in first place (the fact that the work was commissioned by Jeremy Heywood may have been relevant). Traditionally, civil servants served in the background; their names and faces were not widely known, even in Parliament. They were required to serve the government of the day within the law. Governments of all types – Conservative, Liberal, Labour, National, and war-time coalition – relied on them without complaint. The British civil servant developed the habit of serial loyalty.

Over the last forty years that has changed. The modern system of Select Committees began work in 1980. Since then, committee chairs have chipped away at the idea that, because ministers take policy decisions, they have sole responsibility for explaining those decisions. From the beginning, permanent secretaries were called to the fourteen Commons Select Committees to explain how policy had been implemented, and specifically how money had been spent or misspent. But over the years the breadth of questioning has widened. MPs want to know what advice officials offered; they want to dispute policy choices. It is a brave permanent secretary who refers committee members to ministers as the correct target for their questions. And 'target' is the right noun: sessions are increasingly adversarial. The advent of the televising of proceedings in Parliament has changed the atmosphere of evidence sessions. Quite often, when giving evidence, I had the feeling that my questioner was playing to a wider audience. Indeed, sessions with civil servants make the news routinely these days.

Even the intelligence agencies have been swept up in this change. When I started work in 1982, the Secret Intelligence Service, MI5, and GCHQ were not officially avowed; that did not happen until the 1990s, when the head of each agency (and only the head) was named in public. These days agency heads are prominent public figures, giving lectures and interviews. Such appearances are inevitably publicised with the words 'in a rare public appearance', but appearances are now frequent enough for the caveat to be risible. The problems of their being public figures are twofold: appearances whet the appetite – having appeared once, how can further requests (particularly from Parliament) be resisted? And second, some of the helpful mystery around the agencies is dissipated. There is danger in letting daylight in upon magic; what was previously thought to be magical is suddenly revealed as banal. Agency heads would do better to retire again to the shadows.

Other civil servants are not in control of their public appearances. When Parliament calls, they answer. But MPs and peers could remember the distinction between ministers and civil servants: ministers are responsible for policy, civil servants for implementing that policy. The policy-making process is part of the confidential relationship between ministers and civil servants (even freedom of information legislation acknowledges that) and yet 'Did you advise the secretary of state to...' lines of questioning are commonplace.

Publicity and public awareness are not the only disruptors of the traditional undemonstrative and effective relationship between ministers and civil servants. Coinciding with the launch of the modern Select Committee, the BBC broad-cast the first series of *Yes, Minister*, which ran for three seven-episode series from 1980 to 1984 and was followed by *Yes, Prime Minister*, which ran for sixteen episodes from 1986 to 1988. They were funny and popular; famously, they were Margaret Thatcher's favourite TV programme. But they also harmed the Civil Service. The premise, repeated in every episode, was that the civil servant (Sir Humphrey) was always out to get the better of his political master (Jim Hacker). Humphrey was vain, devious, wordy, subtle, determined, and inexhaustible – in a word, wily. Jim was insecure, superficial, vacillating, easily distracted, and whiny – in a word, hapless. Ever since, politicians have half-joked that the series was more a documentary than a sit-com; it planted and nurtured the idea that civil serv-ants had a separate agenda and used their comprehensive knowledge of the system to stymie ministers at every turn. I would never suggest that that was never true but never, in thirty-eight years working in the Civil Service, was it possi-ble to mistake who was working for whom nor who wielded the power, even if in some cases they wielded it poorly or failed to understand how powerful they were.

The second disruptor was *DC Confidential*, a memoir by Christopher Meyer, at the time the recently retired ambas-sador to Washington. Political memoirs and diaries were familiar and predictable. Years ago, *Private Eye* skewered the genre in a couple of sentences; dredging my memory rather than their archive, their parodist wrote something along the lines of: 'I was the cleverest person in the room; I deserved better. Everything since I left has gone horribly wrong; I saw it coming; if only they'd listened to me, disaster could have been averted.' Christopher's was the first memoir by a retired civil servant to court controversy. When certain passages in the book were drawn to his attention, Jack Straw went ballistic. His fury ignited interest: in twenty-four hours, the book went from number 200+ to being in the top ten among Amazon best sellers.

Christopher treated his readers to his unvarnished opinions about ministers who might have expected greater discretion. His book was well written and sold shedloads, the last probably its worst offence in politicians' eyes. Every politician who read it was entitled to wonder whether Christopher's successors were similarly keeping notes with a view to future publication. Instinctive trust has never been assumed since.

I do not kid myself that the genie will retire meekly back into the lamp. The rules governing which material can and cannot be included in books written by retired ministers and civil servants have been stretched by many authors other than Christopher Meyer, but I hope both ministers and civil servants will weigh the consequences of what they publish on those still in the system.

I have four proposals for the Civil Service: first, to reassert the independence of the Civil Service Commission and the impartiality of the process of selecting permanent secretaries and other senior civil servants. These days competitions are habitually rerun if the prime minister and their team are not happy with the shortlist the selection panel offers. My career saw a creeping Americanisation of the Civil Service. The idea of a professional cadre, with deep and prolonged experience in public policymaking, capable of serving governments of any political complexion has been in retreat since the arrival of special advisers in the 1980s. With a flock of SpAds and PAds (policy advisers) at their disposal, ministers rely on civil servants for less and less. They increasingly expect senior civil servants to behave like super SpAds, accepting their agenda without examination. Although civil servants owe their ministerial bosses complete discretion, their ultimate loyalty is to what Douglas Hurd used to call 'the eternal verities': the truth, the law, and value for taxpayers' money. Their advice is offered and disputes are resolved behind closed doors, but they are not doing their job if they unquestioningly implement a minister's agenda.

One key difference between senior officials in the UK and the US is that Americans work only for the Administration that recruits them – all American ambassadors, for example, must offer their resignation to an incoming president. In recent times (Tony Blair's election was a watershed) recruitment of senior civil servants in the UK has increasingly resembled American practice. Too close involvement of ministers in the selection of their senior civil servants might lead opposition politicians to doubt the ability of successful candidates to serve them in due course.

Ministers have always been involved at the end of the process, when a final selection is made among qualified (and ranked) candidates, and they could always feed in their views. After eighteen months at the Foreign Office, with personal knowledge of all the FCO's top team, Lord Carrington asked his PPS to enquire of the PUS's office what plans the PUS had for Julian Bullard, whose work as head of planning staff had impressed him. Latterly, secretaries of state have sought changes in their senior civil servant team more or less on arrival. They lean into selection processes as they start rather than await recommendations.

Secondly, the number of senior civil servants needs to be cut. In times past, most departments had a director-general to cover each of its ministers. That principle could be reasserted as the number of junior ministers reduces.

Thirdly, I propose that, as a cadre, permanent secretaries dispense with the idea of 'starter' permanent secretaryships and others that are usually done by someone who has already been a permanent secretary. The idea is in any case curious because two of the three permanent secretary roles in the great offices of state are generally done by someone in their first such job (Treasury and Foreign Office). In future, the only two jobs where previous perm sec experience is highly desirable could be restricted to cabinet secretary and national security adviser. For the rest, the default setting is that whoever is recruited will not be eligible for any other permanent secretary role in future, except cabinet secretary and national security adviser. Like cabinet ministers, in recent years too many permanent secretaries have been distracted by the prospect of their next job.

Fourthly, having been appointed, permanent secretaries need to do their job for at least five years. Because of the carousel among perm secs, average incumbency has tended to be shorter, usually no more than four years and often under three. The Treasury and Foreign Office are exceptions, where in recent times the perm sec has served for a minimum of five years. After the burst of training jobs at the beginning of a career, other civil servants too could usefully do jobs for longer.

The corollary of doing one permanent secretary job is that candidates need to be focussed on a particular perm sec job rather than the rank, as is sometimes the case right now. Like cabinet jobs, they should not be seen as stepping stones but require the holder's full concentration and sustained effort. Preparation of candidates needs to be tailored to the permanent secretary job they want to do.

In the last few years, we have learned that the Civil Service finds it difficult to defend itself against attack from the top of the system it serves. Some ministers want the Civil Service to be more like business, yet the private and public sectors are fundamentally different. Civil servants are never motivated by profit. They are never trying to enrich themselves; they know that the material benefits of their career choice will not be enviable, will not feature in a glossy magazine, and will not amount to a handsome legacy for their heirs. They know that from the moment they fill in the application form. And they do not care. The rewards are from improving the lives of others, of giving back to a country and community, of leaving country and community a bit stronger because of their work. It is the motivation of a teacher or health care worker, not the motivation of an entrepreneur. Trying to turn civil servants into entrepreneurs has demotivated them and mistaken their vocation. Having a commercial sense (recognising, cherishing, and promoting value for money) is another matter; it is essential, but its promotion has not been the limit of the ambition of some ministers in charge of the civil service.

Like any institution under threat, the Civil Service needs help from outside. It is easier to damage than to repair. Parliament, press, and universities all play a part. I do not know whether the British Civil Service is really the best in the world, but in every country I have worked in it has been studied, admired, and emulated. The most plausible rivals for the laurels are all explicitly based on the British model, in Singapore, New Zealand, Canada, and Australia. Their variations on the British theme stress training, length of service in key jobs and public prestige rather more than the UK does.

In Conclusion

I hope it is clear why I admire British public service. It may not be unique but it is remarkable; it is more vulnerable than those who do not look deeply realise. One of its strengths is explicit recognition of its imperfections and a refusal to accept them as inevitable and ineradicable. Nothing from our history leads us to believe that we will reliably come up with the best answer at the first time of asking. We fail but we are undaunted by failure; we keep trying. Even when things are going well, we try to improve them.

In one of my favourite Mitchell and Webb sketches, the pair are playing Nazi officers. Around them, their fellow officers swagger; it seems the Third Reich is at the peak of its powers. But Mitchell is musing on the details of their uniform, in particular the skull and bones motif: 'Are we the baddies?' British diplomats are always aware of the possibility that we are or were the baddies, perhaps not intentionally, but we know 'I didn't mean it' is not much of a defence. Our predecessors were powerful. We know about Palmerston, gun-boat diplomacy, and the Pax Britannica. We know that we fought and won the shortest war in world history (thirty-eight minutes on the morning of 27 August 1896, against the Sultan of Zanzibar).

Whatever policy area we cover, we also get to know about the casually and invisibly powerful, the Britons known only to specialist historians but who have had a huge and sometimes devastating impact. The Middle East still struggles with the lines Mark Sykes and François Georges-Picot drew in 1916. Less well known is the cartographic contribution of Andrew Ryan, who, while minister at Jeddah in the 1930s, was tasked by George Rendel, his head of department in London, with delineating borders on the Arabian peninsula. When his colleagues discovered Ryan was colour-blind, they obliged him to clarify the lines on his maps with a series of tiny letters: 'b's for blue, 'r's for red, and so on. As this was happening, one of the Persian Gulf sheikhs inquired where the UK considered his territory ended. The acting political resident in the Gulf answered: 'The Southern boundary of Your Highness's dominions is marked by a blue line.' He enclosed no map with his letter. Rendel claimed in his memoir that 'parties on camels went on looking for a blue line in the sands of the desert for several months'. Rendel had wanted to agree borders because geologists had begun prospecting for oil. The India Office opposed him, on the grounds that Abdul Aziz's rule might not last and that, if the UK set rigid limits to areas under its control, it might find itself committed to accepting anarchy across the border. The India Office prevailed and the most lethal disputes, around the Buraimi oasis, persisted, occasionally exploding, from 1949 until 1974.

Sometimes we were the bad guys, even when we did not mean to be and did not know it at the time. But even at its most disputed, the UK's presence left elements of a positive legacy: infrastructure, parliamentary democracy, and regular fair elections, an independent judiciary grounded in common law, the English language, as an additional language which allowed easier communication with the rest of the world. With Israel, the UK's official relationship has been tempestuous at many times since the UK resisted Jewish demands for independence in the 1940s. Prime Minister Sharon's chief of staff delighted in reminding me of controversial episodes. But, having made his point, he recalled in affectionate detail what the British mandate had done for the State of Israel. In 2003 he reminded me that until the Ben Gurion Airport 2000 project, the British had built all functioning airports in the country, 'indeed, you can still make that boast' (the new terminal eventually opened in October 2004). The institutions he liked (his boss less so) – the Supreme Court and the office of the Attorney-General – had British roots. In international relations, if it is important, it tends to be complicated.

I spent all my adult life dealing with the UK's international relations. At the end of my career as much as at the beginning we spent most of our time thinking about hard power, the sort of power that feels most within the control of states, tending alliances, deploying forces, and threatening consequences (economic and personal more often than military) if another state did something we disapproved of strongly enough. Hard power still counts. What China is doing in the South China Sea is all about hard power. Russian troops devastating Ukraine is hard power. Yet for a country of the UK's size, decisive hard power is a memory and an illusion. Sometimes others will share that illusion (if only for a time) and hard power will feel real again, but the era when British hard power shaped events is over.

British power is still real, even if its nature disappoints some parliamentarians. It is soft power. It is the power of example. Because of our language and our history, more people around the world know what is happening in the UK. British culture and sport maintain a global reach. British ceremonial and the British response in times of global trouble still command global attention. The world still principally uses English courts for arbitration. The soft power of our institutions, our universities, our media, and the City of London maintains our international relevance.

One of the UK's most important institutions, global in its influence, is the BBC. One of its three core Reithian values has become, almost by accident, a global mission. Lord Reith aimed 'to educate, inform and entertain'; all three tasks were always shared. These days two are widely shared to everyone's benefit. But others seeking to inform are not doing as good a job. News organisations under the control of a state or a profit-maximising businessperson are less wedded to the facts and can be explicitly political in their editorial decisions.

The BBC's unique selling point is getting facts right, on all subjects, in all places, and at all times. Gorbachev listened to the BBC World Service in the basement of his dacha in Crimea during the failed coup in Russia in 1991. He later told the British ambassador that that was the only way he could tell what was really happening in Moscow. The BBC's mistakes are rare and quickly corrected. The world respects the BBC's reputation for accuracy, which gives them access other news organisations envy and an audience which continues to grow despite proliferating competition, reaching 468 million people every week, in forty-two languages. As the twenty-first century wears on, it is increasingly clear that accuracy is not enough for it to preserve its reputation or carry out its role; editorial choices – what to cover, in what order, with what thoroughness, and in what context – are vitally important. A fully independent, well-resourced BBC, able to cover news in every country of the world, holding itself to the highest standards of honesty and impartiality, is a British service to the world.

Three global challenges haunt the world in the middle of the twenty-first century, their newness and their scale meaning that collectively we are not close yet to gripping them: the environment, information technology, and the truth. Our planet cannot survive eleven billion human beings if human beings do not fundamentally change their behaviour towards the planet. The possibilities of new technologies are limitless, for bad as well as good; we have to decide the limits of technology's control on our lives. And facts are precious: if a government controls the facts, it controls its population. In 2020, the Chinese ambassador to the UK went on the BBC's *Andrew Marr Show*. The ministry in Beijing that sanctioned the appearance forgot that British journalists do not allow interviewees to vet the questions. Halfway through the interview, Marr confronted Liu Xiaoming with images, taken by a BBC crew in the Xinjiang province at the invitation of the Chinese authorities, and asked about the repression of Uighurs, seen obediently on screen chanting the virtues of the Chinese way. Liu was flummoxed. Totalitarian regimes reveal their nature when trying to convince outsiders of the benefits of their way of doing things; what works for them never works for an audience that is not dependent on them.

The best ideas rather than the biggest armies will count for most in the second half of the twenty-first century, and the UK can be the generator or the location of ideas for tackling climate change, protecting biodiversity, and for inventing and regulating new technology. The UK can also be a laboratory for transformative policies that affect relatively small numbers of people: Liam Fox's work in 2022 to secure passage of the Down Syndrome Act, the first legislation anywhere in the world focused on helping people with Down Syndrome, is one example.

The testimony of others is more persuasive than our own about the excellence of our performance. Before I joined the House of Lords, I had taken part in only two debates. The first was at De La Salle; I was about thirteen years old. I cannot remember the subject, but I do remember I was seconding the proposition. I wrote out everything I wanted to say, we lost, and the judges warned me not to gabble. The second was at Tel Aviv University. I was supporting Natan Sharansky, who was minister without portfolio at the time, trying to dissuade the student jury from endorsing the proposition that 'The British have done more harm than good in the world.'

I was intrigued that Sharansky had agreed to speak against the proposition. It quickly became apparent why. He was born Anatoly Shcharansky in 1948 in Donetsk (then Stalino), the son of a journalist. In the 1970s, he became one of the Soviet Union's highest profile refuseniks, campaigning for human rights and the right of Jews to emigrate. In 1977, he was arrested, charged with treason and, in 1978, sentenced to thirteen years forced labour. He was not a quiet prisoner, repeatedly staging hunger strikes to draw attention to the plight of Soviet political prisoners. In 1986, he benefited from an exchange of prisoners, in the process becoming the first to be released by Mikhail Gorbachev.

Sharansky recounted the story of his deportation. On 11 February 1986, he was flown to Berlin and found himself on the eastern side of the Glienicke Bridge, connecting Wannsee and Potsdam. Snow lay on the ground. In front of him, in the west, Sharansky could see the welcoming party. The last thing his Soviet handlers told him was, 'Go straight, go quick, don't look back; if you deviate, we'll shoot.' He recalled, 'I was damned if I was going to let them dictate to me at the end; so I took as long and meandering a route as I could, shuffling through the snow. I knew they wouldn't shoot.' The exit fixed Glienicke as the bridge of spies (celebrated in Steven Spielberg's film), but Sharansky's exit was one of only three times the bridge was used for a Cold War prisoner exchange. By the evening of the day of his deportation, he was already in Israel.

Twenty years later, Sharansky told the student audience how he had kept going in the gulag. His warders hated the fact that he wanted to leave their country. They tormented him with evidence of the weakness and failure of the West. The UK was a particular bugbear. Every day they read aloud long extracts from the *Morning Star*, the UK's daily Communist newspaper. 'You see what these people are really like? You see how feeble they are? This is the place you admire? You would exchange the country of your birth for this?'

By now Sharansky had the student audience in the palm of his hand. 'Yes,' he told them, 'Yes, I thought every day. Yes, because this is what freedom looks like. Of course, the British government dispute every word and hate it being said. But the point is that they allow it to be said.' More than anything, Sharansky wanted to enjoy that freedom himself.

The students were impressed. We won the debate.

Index